Protestation

In all that I shall say in this book I submit to what is taught by Our mother, the Holy Roman Church; if there is anything in it contrary to this, it will be without my knowledge. Therefore, for the love of our Lord, I beg the learned men who are to read it to look at it very carefully and to make known to me any faults of this nature which there may be in it and the many others which it will have of other kinds. If there is anything good in it, let this be to the glory and honor of God in the service of His most sacred Mother, our Patroness and Lady.[1]

Kennedy Hall
meaningofcatholic.com/contact

---

[1] Adapted from the protestation given by St. Teresa of Avila in *Way of Perfection*

By the same author

Terror of Demons: Reclaiming Traditional Catholic
Masculinity

Lockdown with the Devil

Kennedy Hall

LOCKDOWN WITH THE DEVIL

KENNEDY HALL

ISBN 978-0-578-37510-6

Our Lady of Victory Press is an imprint of The Meaning of Catholic.

The Meaning of Catholic is a lay apostolate dedicated to uniting Catholics against the enemies of Holy Church.

MeaningofCatholic.com

Graphic design and layout by W. Flanders.

Our Lady of Victory, pray for us!

This book is a work of fiction. We have endeavoured to ensure that all theological propositions are orthodox. However, various symbolic images or literary devices are used at times to transmit the messages relevant to the story. We are certain there are no objective theological errors herein, nonetheless it is useful to keep in mind the artistic intent of the work.

Acknowledgements

Thank you to Timothy Flanders and his wife Whitney for all the work you have done in helping me publish this book. Tim especially, without your efforts in editing and critiquing, I am certain this work would not be as successful.

To Don and Dave, my cup of Chimay doth run over.

Kennedy Hall
Our Lady of Victory
Anno Domini MMXX

A time will come when the decisive battle between the kingdom of Christ and Satan will be over marriage and the family.

–Sister Lucia, Seer of Fatima

When Mary has struck her roots in a soul, she produces there marvels of grace, which she alone can produce.

–True Devotion to Mary, Saint Louis de Montfort

I

Malthus my boy,

Administration has informed me of my obligation in forming and guiding yet another junior devil. I am sure you are familiar with this relationship, and have no doubt heard of what happens to novices who miss the mark: if you prove incompetent and fail in your endeavour, I will have my way with you. Let this be a firm reminder.

The humans are under the impression that we "work together" to uphold this lowerarchy and to fill our Father's house. They foolishly assume that we share some "common goal," like they do when faced with a task. If there is any manner of working with one another, it is the way scavenging birds work together. Souls are food, nothing more and nothing less, therefore I will tolerate this assignment as a means to an end. Secure your endeavours by following my advice, and perhaps you may avoid a fate common to those arrogant devils who forget their station.

The Enemy is no fool, and his so-called "Guardians," the ghastly messengers He employs to protect His disgusting creatures, work just as hard as we do. Now, these Guardians are in reality cowards, which was evidenced at their pitiful obedience to the Enemy when our Father Below so courageously rejected the unjust contractual demands presented to him at the beginning of time. Nonetheless, they are formidable opponents, and they do not play fair. They always seem to have insider information from the Enemy's camp. As of yet we have not figured out how this is so.

However, we expect that with continued progress of the Innovation Task Force, we will soon crack the code to this trickery, and therefore level the playing field.

In any case, The Cabinet tells me that you show great potential, and has thus tasked you with the oversight of an entire family. Of course, you will still have at your disposal the lesser devils who will torment the unique members of the family, but you are charged with orchestrating the whole affair. In former times, we would not entrust so much responsibility to such a junior tempter, but, the humans are more spiritually weak than they have ever been. The majority of them have so completely given up on the Enemy, that we have never before enjoyed such a surplus of souls at our infernal banquet. If it were possible, I might even say that I was satisfied with this continual harvest. Of course, we will never be satisfied if even a single soul escapes our grasp, as it is a wholly unjust reality that the Enemy believes He has a "right" to his so-called children.

The family under your charge is what they call a "modern" family. I never tire of how these humans think they can simply add a descriptive word, believing it changes the reality of a thing. The word "modern" is perhaps one of our greatest assets, for it can be used to trick our patients into allying themselves with even the most absurd of ideas. The human family is the primordial unit that our Father Below so eloquently attacked in that ancient Garden, and nothing about it has changed in the slightest since then. However, most humans are convinced that so-called "modernity" means that their family unit is somehow different from that of their First Parents. They are currently so gullible that they believe the passage of time changes the nature of what is eternally true, as if something could be ontologically different on Thursday than it was on Tuesday. Just as it was at the beginning, families are where the humans develop. So our task is to corrupt the unit as much as possible, and in this way ensure their entrance into our kingdom.

The sort of relativism needed for them to view the nature of the family as a changeable thing, is no doubt the result of our past endeavours. Not least of our efforts has been the notion of Evolutionary Theory. You see, we have implanted in their collective philosophies, through the efforts of our most dedicated disciples, the idea that the nature of the created realm is in a state of flux. Many of them believe that they share some common bestial ancestor, and that through millions of unseen years they have somehow arrived at their current state. Inherent to this idea is the proposition that only the "fittest" survive, which is quite amusing as only the unfit minds of the current civilization believe such a splendid lie. Since they see their nature as being in continual adaptation and even radical transformation to their environment, it only follows that the family would also adapt. As a result, the fools now accept as an inevitable reality all manner of familial dysfunction as a mere sign of the times, or evidence of a changing world. I say, when this tactic was proposed at a meeting of strategists centuries ago, even I had my doubts, thinking the vermin were at least intelligent enough to avoid such an obvious farce. Nonetheless, I was delighted to be proved wrong.

I see no reason why your family should be any different than the vast majority currently are. If there was any real threat of resistance, surely we would not be entrusting a rookie such as yourself. Fortunately, it is rare to find a family that gives us any reason to do anything other than throw inexperienced devils at them.

Until I receive more reconnaissance information from you and your underlings, I cannot give you specific advice as to how you may destroy this particular family. But, not much has changed in our line of work, and the "old tricks" still work, even if a minor tweak in operative procedure is required. I imagine that the father is not much different from most modern patriarchs, little concerned with the spiritual fabric of his family. The patriarchs are the fountain heads of the family, and therefore must be our primary target. If the man is weak we can take him directly, if he is strong then we must go around him to the women and children. All of them have chinks in their armour, and this man should be no different. It is probable that he himself will offer us various fleshly weaknesses that we can exploit. It is simply a matter of encouraging him to look at those nauseating images of souls engaging in that horrendous activity the Enemy reserves for marriage. More on this tactic in a later correspondence, but be assured of its efficacy in trapping specimens for our bidding. Start by curating his viewing habits on his electronic machines in our direction, ensuring that the content is of the brutal and sexualized sort that permeates all popular programming for adults these days.

Until next time,

Quelle

II

Malthus my boy,

I have received the dossier on your specimens, and although it was tardy and should have been handed in sooner—do not let that happen again—it is informative enough for now. Alas, the father does not as of yet have a habit of utilizing sexualized imagery for his own purposes, however, there is still time and much else with which to work. It seems that this family is typical of their age. What they now call the "Western World," which is in reality the remnants of Christendom, is filled with this sort of affair. As usual, we have for ourselves the statistically normative unit of two parents and two children, no doubt the result of neutering.

I tell you, the fact that we worked so hard to foment a sterile spirit of neutering into their world has for us proven to be both positive and negative. On the one hand, the fact that the humans have for the most part adopted the practice of limiting their family size has been of great benefit for us. For the first time in human history, the majority of them view sexual activity as a completely relative affair; they decide on their own terms how they wish to partake, with the procreation of more humans as an afterthought or inconvenience. Even many of the Christians have reconciled this idea, apparently forgetting that the Enemy clearly warns against it in His Scriptures. It seems as if Onan being struck down was not a clear enough example as to what is expected of his creatures in marriage.

On the other hand, despite the delightful fact that the sterile mentality has of course encouraged untold amounts of them to lust, there are less souls for us to hunt as there are less children conceived. As of yet we have not figured how to encourage them to have large families while at the same time encouraging sexual licentiousness.

Because of the sterile mentality, most families now view their lives in little cookie-cutter stages. That is, they plan in their minds a life that has but a few years with small children, and therefore look at those tiresome times as a hurdle to be surmounted, as if it were an obligatory burden. Often you will even hear the lemmings parrot the same responses to anyone who informs them of a new pregnancy. If the offspring are born in a smaller window of time than is average, you may hear "Oh good, have them close together, this way they will all be young at the same time." Or, it is also common to happen upon statements like, "Oh congratulations, you're done right?"

Every time I hear them speak like this, I am giddy. Because of contraception, the furthering of their species is now such a mundane reality in their minds that they speak about their progeny as if they are collectible trinkets or a task to be completed like filing their income tax. As a result, they have now forgotten both the sacrificial character their ancestors earned from having larger families, as well as the youthful vigour that the nauseant laughter of small children gives even to the old. Why they find such ridiculous pleasure in the involuntary vocal inflections of their younger offspring, I will never understand.

From what you tell me of this family, they fit the mold perfectly. Both parents find themselves comfortably in the early part of their forties, with one child in the midst of, and the other approaching adolescence. The parents are superficially wealthy, but in reality have accrued large amounts of debt, nonetheless they are pleased with their materialist comforts. Since they now view themselves as out of their "small children years," they now claim they are helping their son and daughter become more independent. In reality, they are doing everything they can to be independent from their own children. What with the constant sporting events, dropping off at the homes of friends—friends with suspect morals the parents have not inquired into—and numerous lessons and extracurricular activities; they spend a mere two hours or less all awake and together under the same roof at the same time each day. Of course on weekends they are together for more so-called "quality time," however this time seems to be spent like most other families, filled with social engagements and copious amounts of time staring at individually catered screens.

It is not all good news you tell me. The father did insist years ago that they put their children through religious schools. Now, we have had arguably as much or more success in these schools as any, however, there are still opportunities for the Enemy to present himself to the creatures in these environments. Unfortunately, you tell me that the eldest, the boy, has recently been inspired by a teacher who professes the Truth the Enemy demands. The young man is now growing ever more curious and finds himself asking probing questions to his instructor, a man who is regrettably orthodox.

There is no reason to worry, as the rest of the boy's experiences in his community are just as irreligious as anywhere else. But, we mustn't grow complacent either as the Enemy works in an entirely non mathematical manner; He is able to wipe a soul clean of accumulated sins as if they never happened. At any moment he may ignite an insatiable urge for heavenly things in the young man as a result of what he hears in his classroom. There is nothing we can do at the moment about the teacher, as he seems to be solidly in the Enemy camp, however, we can influence how the parents react to the information being spread in the classroom. Most parents today feign any real interest in their children's education. They are above all concerned with results that meet the artificial standards of the system. In addition, most parents who send their offspring to religious schools do not actually believe the religion. They instead adhere to some caricature of the faith that they have pieced together in their minds from their own watered down education. Their children could be taught all manner of inspired heresy, and they would never have a clue. In fact, as long as the heresy seems to blend with the societal obsession with political correctness, the dimwitted parents will often conclude that the Church has even changed her teachings; something we know is impossible, no matter our efforts. The small minority of parents who do object to the heretical education of their children are dealt with accordingly. They are labeled by faculty members and other parents as "extremists," "fundamentalists" and, my personal favourite: "radical traditionalists."

Until we speak again, continue the usual barrage of petty and decadent temptations at the mother and father. It has been decades since either of them have meaningfully reconciled their consciences with the Enemy, which means they should fold quite nicely with a bit of pressure.

Until next time,

Quelle

III

Malthus my boy,

I see you are continuing with the trickle of simple temptations at the mother and father, and they seem to be doing the job, for now. Constant video watching and electronic networking provides sufficient distraction for both of them. The woman is evidently open to an onslaught of what they call "reality TV," which is in fact nothing more than a popular form of idol worship and gossip. When children witness their parents partake in such infantile pass times, they learn through a type of environmental osmosis that when they are older, they can recreate with meaningless distractions that are somehow reserved for when they are mature.

One of our most effective tricks has been to partition the supposed morality of films and other media by applying grades of maturity and guidance. Young children watch things that their parents believe are approved for their age, and as they age, the grip of supervision is gradually lifted. The family will watch an appropriate film together before the little ones are off to bed, and they reserve the "rated R" movies for adult time. This shows the children that as they age, all the immoral and hellishly good behaviour their parents warn them of actually becomes the basis for all their entertainment. Whether they are conscious of it or not, parents for decades now have tacitly approved of all forms of sexual deviance, drug use and criminal violence by reserving the "mature" films for themselves. In reality, since the parents of this age are the feeblest of perhaps any in history, young pubescents now engage in the smut and waste that parents of just a decade or two ago would have hidden from them. Fathers especially love to facilitate this, most notably when they give their young sons a "treat"—a treat for us no doubt—by sharing with them the experience of their first grown-up film. Thinking they are doing a favour for their boys, they are in reality doing a favour for us as they expose the boy to a world of glorified promiscuity and a lust for violence. Is it any wonder why most men are defenceless against the temptations of the flesh?

However, I am pained to hear that you cannot engender a habit of pornographic images in the husband. This is actually quite rare, as most men outside the Enemy's camp at least dabble in the disgusting behaviour on a regular basis. Unfortunately, it seems as if this couple has cultivated an abhorrent level of trust in their marriage. The woman at one point strongly suggested to her husband that it would "break her heart" if he partook in that activity which guarantees us such a voluminous banquet. This man represents the most hypocritical and weak-kneed sort of weasel we encounter; he desires to indulge in animalistic imagery, but refrains only to appease his wife. His mind wanders to any place we guide it, yet he has not the courage to do what he wants—it is pathetic. Men like him are never able to abstain permanently from the activities we want. It is a matter of time before we are able to hammer into his skull the reality that he is the most shameful of pests. Just wait—when he finally does acquiesce to the call of pornography, he will acclimate nicely to that demonic crescendo that exalts his perversion in vile ambrosia, and he will see himself for the slave he truly is.

Thankfully, due to our voracious endeavours of the last century, most schools and churchmen have been robbed of their traditional teachings on the metaphysical reality of the human person. Because of this, they have no way of understanding how they sin with their bodies. You see, their souls are in fact the form of their bodies, which means that what they do with their bodies will affect their souls. Given the fact that their metacognitive faculties are housed in their souls, they cannot think clearly when the soul is sick. Therefore, we must ensure that every disgusting behaviour and perversion is encouraged, thereby transitioning a soul from a pool of clear water into a veritable latrine of deviant defecation. Remember: their sinfulness increases their stupidity. This stupidity does not necessarily apply to their practical intelligence, however they do in fact become morally unintelligent.

It is in a way quite pitiful, as men will swear to an exasperated wife that they will never partake in the filthy behaviour, yet, when push comes to shove, they have no moral resistance. Knowing full well what the consequences may be as a result of such delinquency, they still pursue the shameful habit in secret. With the advent of modern mobile devices, it is almost no fun to consider how easily we can facilitate a frequent dabbling in this animalistic dereliction. The phrase "shooting fish in a barrel" comes to mind.

At any rate, this man, for whatever reason, has a stronger conscience than is ideal, but he is not invincible. He does not fully understand why he should refrain from the activity, but he does seem to commit himself to such a sappy love and admiration for his spouse, that he will not cross her wishes for the time being. There are two ways to use a situation like this to our advantage. The first is to convince the woman that she is being unreasonable by demanding such restraint from him, and that if she were to encourage him to partake she would be helping to meet his needs. Women who acquiesce to this usually do so against their own will, and are continually disgusted with themselves for doing so. Furthermore, women who take this approach will often indulge with the husband, which is useful for us as it makes her an adulteress just like her husband. Often we are able to parlay this behaviour into full marital infidelity. Increasingly, many wives do take this approach, as they have been conditioned to view their husbands as apelike perverts, while at the same time still vying for their approval and admiration. *Your desire shall be for your husband, and he shall rule over you...* The second approach seems to fit our situation, as it seems that your woman has held firm to her anti-pornography position. In a situation like this, it is necessary to focus strictly on the moral resolve of the man, so when he does finally give in and the woman eventually discovers this fact—they always discover this fact—then the husband will appear a cruel monster who has lived a double life. Pornography is adultery, plain and simple, therefore all we must do is amplify whichever form of adultery we are offered, whether that be the internal or external forum.

In the meantime, something must be done about the messages being transmitted from that blasted teacher to their son. The boy has now become completely convinced of the philosophical reality of the Enemy and the historical certainty of the Resurrection of the Awesome and Terrible Name. To put it mildly, is not favourable to our efforts. In my experience, once a person has been fully convinced of these truths, although we may encourage him to ignore them, they can never truly forget. When a human is convinced of the truth of that historical event 2000 years ago, we are at a disadvantage indeed.

The boy is still not regularly frequenting the Sacraments. He is therefore relying on the particular graces being offered him, and still does not enjoy the steadfast foundation that the Enemy's instruments afford the spiritual life. It is true that at the moment his "mind is blown" (ugh) by the things he is learning, but we have duped many a young man into our camp after he has enjoyed a brief reprieve on the other side.

We have so diligently chipped away at the objectivity of truth in all levels of education, which means that what this teacher is offering his students is simultaneously attractive and offensive. The truth of which the Enemy speaks is unavoidably real when it is heard, which also means that it can be startling. The world we have facilitated, not just for the youth, is a world of relativistic fantasy, rife with electronic friendships and an utter avoidance of reality. Therefore, when they come in contact with the message from our opposition, it is as if a man who has breathed smoke for decades is now taking in a gulp of mountain air. They may be pleased by it, however, it is hard to take. The work we have done has made their souls into veritable moral and philosophical paraplegics, thus many prefer to remain paralyzed than to take the first agonizing step out of hellish comfort.

For now we cannot convince the boy otherwise, at least on an intellectual level, as we have no means to defeat the opposing arguments. Nonetheless, presently you should focus your efforts and the efforts of your subservient devils on turning the boy's friends against him. Since we invented the term "teenager" as a method to remove adolescents from responsibility (no doubt thanks to great efforts around the Great War) the need to conform to the fashions of the "peer" group has been a most useful instrument for us. Ensure that those around the boy remark at just how "judgmental" he has now become due to his nascent Christian belief. Let us see if we cannot use social pressures to shame the young man into submission.

Until next time,

Quelle

IV

Malthus my boy,

I must say, I am pleased with your last report. It seems as if you have not only engendered severe opposition to the beliefs of the young man by his peers, but you have also fomented a campaign of lies and deceit against the educator. This is very good news. We must be realistic, it is improbable that we will move the man from his position; his devotion to the Woman is too strong. However, with the application of fanatical political correctness, we can fan the flames of the mob mentality against the instructor. In the past, we could only hope for isolated groups of people to gather in mobs with pitch-forks and torches. But now, as humans begin to remove themselves even further from actual lived reality, they are easily manipulated by the most illogical and absurd phraseology and slogans shared throughout their virtual platforms.

These tools are useful in making the public and professional lives of the targets of the cyber mob most unpleasant. But men who are devoted to the Enemy unfortunately look at things from a supernatural perspective, and therefore tend to rejoice in their public sufferings as a way to partake in the humiliation suffered by the Son of the Enemy. It enrages me that the opposition has co-opted even suffering as something worthwhile! Fortunately the materialist worldview that now occupies the collective psyche of whole nations has all but rejected the notion of suffering as having any benefit.

In ages gone by, we had to work quite hard to convince large groups of people of falsity and to enrage their sensibilities against an innocent person. Presently, we can influence droves of persons under our care in ways that facilitate a constant stream of arbitrary lies that detract from any man's character. It is not even remotely necessary that the messages contain any truth, as most humans do not verify their information any more. All that is needed is a catchy sentence or series of capitalized words. As long as a man is labeled a "bigot" or as having a certain "phobia," we can practically tar and feather him with no effort.

We are able to turn children against their parents and even their entire ancestry as a result of these methods. Since the perceived truth of the culture changes with every passing moment, it is inevitable that parents will have "outdated" beliefs. A mother may raise her children to believe that it is a good thing to go to Church on Sundays, or for her daughters to act feminine. But, when her daughter comes home from our inspired university lectures, or has found a community of "progressives" on the internet, she will grow to resent her mother as a cog in the machine of the Patriarchy. Since most mothers cannot stand to have their children think poorly of them, they will reconcile to themselves that they are in fact still in the process of "working through" the old ways by which they were raised, ways that were somehow "repressive." In the best of cases, mothers will even adopt the views and fashions of their brainwashed daughters, and soon they will think and act as they do.

The offspring view these changes in their parents with great affection, and will even say things like, "my mom is so cool, she doesn't impose any of her beliefs on me, she lets me decide for myself." Do you see how stupid this is? The Enemy has designed the family as an institution wherein parents will form their children by way of teaching various lessons. To say it is a good thing that a parent not "impose"—which in reality means to teach—is like saying it is a good thing that a music instructor never informed a student how to read music. Furthermore, children from families like this will, to our great pleasure, inevitably become depressed in some fashion, and therefore grow to resent their parents as the supposed cause of all their trauma. We now have so many aspects of familial destruction so excellently booby-trapped that in some cases all we must do is watch. Do you now see how to use these advances in your attack?

As effective as these methods are, they require the population to have a type of blood-lust for shaming people with which they disagree. This is of course useful, but because most humans are like unintelligent predatory animals, they will not expend more effort than is needed, and are often distracted by easier prey. We need the humans to be easily distracted in order to lead them in whatever direction we desire. But the ease with which they are pulled in any direction also means they have very little resolve and practically no attention span. It is most frustrating. Often we will stick a group of them on an individual, but in their primitive pursuit they will even turn on each other, like buzzards fighting over a rotting carcass. It is the cost of doing business it seems.

It is inevitable that the parents of the students in the boy's class will begin to commiserate about the meddlesome teacher, no doubt due to his "outdated beliefs." This will ensure that the parents of the family under your care look more deeply into what their son now believes. As of yet, they are still unaware of any real changes in their son, although they may have noticed him reading more and spending less time with his peers. Have the mother and father participate in salacious and calumnious conversations about the boy's educator. This way, they will work themselves into a fit, and when they finally confront the child under the guise of "concern," they will in effect seem like they are attacking the young man's newfound faith by associating it with a man they so clearly dislike; a man they have never spoken to. The boy will be distraught that his mother and father so unfairly hate what he believes, without an ounce of understanding of what he truly believes; and the parents will convince themselves that they are "losing" their son due to his emotional defence of his position and the teacher they hate so much.

The psychological effects of this will almost guarantee that the parents will view the instructor as their enemy. They will even start throwing around terms like "brainwashing" when they think of the effect he is having on their child. It is unlikely they will ever speak with him, which is to our benefit, and due to the lack of tact and courage in most, they may even send him a message of correspondence filled with hastily written words they would never dare say in person. They, like most of their peers, are cowards of the highest degree.

Whatever you do, keep the parents from actually speaking with him. He is too convincing and even likeable. We must discourage any real personal encounters with any sort of person devoted to the Enemy, especially since it is likely that men of his ilk will even pray for those who persecute him. It makes me sick.

Until next time,

Quelle

V

Malthus my boy,

The conversation between the boy and his parents went just as I suspected. No real information was learned by the parents as they had already made up their minds beforehand. Furthermore, the boy is now experiencing significant doubts about his beliefs, especially since his father was able to throw a series of emotionally charged questions and accusations at him, to which the young man could not respond. I am glad to see that the father is so unoriginal in his thought that he put forth the same tired objections that virtually all gullible and unintelligent men do in these circumstances.

Almost as if following a script we had written for him he said, "How can you hold so fast to a belief system that has no scientific basis?" And perhaps the most disingenuous yet sanctimonious of all, "The Church mistreats women, how can you look at your mother and sister in the eye and say you believe in a Church that does not have equality for women?" I must admit it tickled me when I heard the words "science" and "equality." The list of meaningless words that the lemmings use to pretend they are sophisticated is so predictable.

There is nothing unique about any of these statements, and the father does not really believe them himself. He, like virtually all humans, does not even know what he means when he appeals to "science," as he is not himself a scientist, and even scientists work with a very limited understanding relative to the infinitely complex nature of the Enemy's creation. Due to popular documentary videos and various celebrity "scientists" we have convinced the humans that the natural sciences can explain anything and everything. Matters of historical fact? They appeal to scientists rather than written testimonies of their ancestors. The existence of the Enemy? They claim there is no "scientific proof" for His existence, all the while not realising the faulty logic inherent to a claim that since you cannot see a supernatural reality under a microscope, that it must not exist. They are so daft and gullible that they hang on every word that drools out of the mouth of anyone in a white lab coat. They pretend they are advanced and in a state of material progress as they do obeisance to a veritable priesthood of scientific magicians, who like the pagan wizards of old promise them the secret to immortality with potions and incantations.

They even trust the scientists with such blindness that many of them have bought into the lie that they can even control the climate of the Earth. Oh yes, they have stated that a change in drinking straw material will change the fate of the natural world. They are morons. It is incredible how utterly unscientific they have become, and how zealous they are for a pseudoscientific and superstitious worldview.

Here is one of the truths we work so tirelessly to keep hidden: the greater their belief in the Enemy, the more reasonable and logical they become. We must continually encourage them to believe with all their pompous certainty that the amorphous concept of scientific vaguery is the key to understanding all that matters in life. All the while they can continue in their materialist worship of creatures and created things, ignoring the fact that they are not an ounce happier than their ancestors, who lived a simpler life that was filled with devotion to the Enemy and less "scientific progress."

In the past we weren't sure whether it was beneficial to encourage a materialist point of view in all cases, given the fact that although a materialist does not believe in the Enemy, he also does not believe in devils. However, since the lines of natural scientific thought and preternatural consultation have been so pleasantly blurred, we can now trick a man into belief in distinctly metaphysical "forces" and "energies." Even men, and not just women, are more frequently consulting eastern gurus and practitioners in an attempt to align their bodies with the "forces of the universe." Just like that the Vessel of Election wrote two thousand years ago, they have now begun to worship the creature, and therefore the Enemy has given them up to base and wholly unnatural desires. It is a sight to behold my boy!

In addition, the father's statement about the equality of women as regards the Church is par for the course these days. Human beings are so far removed from the fact that they have been created male and female, with distinct purpose and abilities, that they view any natural difference as "inequality." It is delightful to watch as they completely miss the point when they suggest that women will only have equality in the Church when they can be a priest.

The work that the Language Redefinition Department has done to void words of any real meaning has been quite effective. For example, the word "equality" means to most of them that they should get whatever they want, even if it makes no sense. They now believe that a sign of so-called equality is apparent when a woman can act in a role that is called Father.

Here is yet another secret about which we do not want them to wise up: the further they flee from the Enemy and towards us, the less value they actually have for their women. The Church has always held that the act of procreation, although appalling to us, is a partaking in the Divine Creation through which a woman has a unique and inimitable role. In fact, the place of a woman is seen so highly in the Enemy's eyes that the Mother of the Son is venerated above all human beings by orders of infinite magnitude. Whatever you do, do not allow any member of this family to understand this fact, and you must keep devotion to the Woman as far from their consciousness as possible. She is… well, just keep the thought of her from them.

At any rate, men now convince themselves that they are "honouring" women by suggesting they should do things men were created to do, thereby abandoning what is true to their feminine nature. In reality, the pretense of honouring the females is nothing more than a pathetic projection of their own gnawing guilt. They know they are scum, what with their endless collections of nude images and videos, and the hours spent hiding in a closet like a rat obsessing over rotted flesh. They are even convinced that having less children and even terminating their own offspring is somehow a "woman's right," as if clipping the wings of an eagle makes the creature more of a bird. It is now socially acceptable to bed a woman, find out she is with child, and then "support" her in her decision to terminate. All the while the vast majority of progressive men shrug their effeminate shoulders as they claim it really is "her choice." Men who speak like this are such hypocrites, and it is music to my ears (hypocrisy is hellishly good).

Well, it seems as if this operation has the proper trajectory, a textbook case. Before I forget, I have been informed that we are to instruct our underlings to pay attention to the virus that has caught the attention of the humans. Stay tuned.

Until next time,

Quelle

VI

Malthus my boy,

I admit that I myself was not privy to the extent of the work being done by our Propaganda Department in preparation for the contagion that is now gripping the minds of the human race. I should have by now received a promotion to a higher post wherein I would be informed of such information, but it seems that the petulant weasels on the Hiring Committee are unjust in their assessment of my skills. I will have my revenge however. Oh, do not dare repeat any of this, I will of course deny it, and since I am still in charge of your career, I will destroy you if need be. One bad review from me and I will have you relegated to the Maintenance Committee, cleaning up the debris from all the fun our torturers have with the damned, without ever partaking yourself.

As of yet, it is not clear to them whether or not the virus is all that serious to the actual welfare of the human race, given that they always die from a myriad of diseases anyway. No matter, we are not concerned if it is serious or not, we can use it to our advantage either way. Truthfully, the ideal scenario is one wherein the vermin are manipulated into a fearful panic, only to avoid an illness that does not "live up to the hype." I already hear talk of "lockdowns" and "nationwide quarantines," all due to the guidance of a select few government bureaucrats who in some way exercise more power over the fate of nations than even the Heads of State.

This generation of humans in the lands formerly Christian are morally speaking, dreadful cowards. The remote chance of dying at an age or in a manner they did not themselves imagine will send most of them into a frantic tizzy. They have become so accustomed to the novel idea that they would be best to die at a nice old age, surrounded by loved ones, and in their sleep. Of course, this does happen for some, but they fail to realize that the less they are encouraged to contemplate death, the more room we have to work away at their souls. The comfort they now widely enjoy, a reality that pleases us very much, is a fertile breeding ground for despair; a fruitful soil for the harvest of Hell.

It is true that the Enemy created them originally without the sting of bodily death, however since He is always bending the rules in His favour, death is now one of His greatest assets. He promises them eternity with Him so long as they die in a State of Grace, reconciled to His laws. In ages past, death was more acutely present at the forefront of their thoughts. This meant that even the impious and religiously disinterested among them could not help but entertain that nagging prick in a soiled conscience that there may be fires in Hell after all. But, through a combination of numbing medication, artificially contrived life expectancies, and the promise of things like "dying with dignity"—which in reality means being put down like a sick animal—we are now able to convince the human animals that any "premature" death is unjust. How fun!

What fools, there is no death that is premature, as the Enemy, always seeking to be in control, has numbered their days! They cannot go a moment sooner than He permits, yet daily we can assure these weaklings that with enough medicine and technology, *they can become like gods*. Our Father Below really did hatch the greatest plan when he tricked the first progenitors that they could have their cake and eat it too. Due to the effects of this original fall, we can always tempt the lemmings to consider grasping at a forbidden, yet fleeting shadow of immortality. They willingly forgo their inheritance in the Enemy's Fortress, only to fall even deeper. Oh happy fall indeed.

Taking into account all that I have heretofore explained, we have an excellent opportunity to foment chaos and confusion amongst them as the hysteria of this contagion grips the collective consciousness of their "developed" world. This should be easily done with your family. Their dependency on electronic communication, especially on the devices they carry with them at all times, means that we will have their gazes fixed on numbers of deaths and infections without any context for what the numbers even mean. The globalized nature of instant and unyielding social media means nations and governments of all stripes will pressure their citizens into policing each other by way of shame and gossip. As they watch unreliable statistics about the virus compound like numbers from a professional sporting event, many of them will spiral into a state of constant hysteria.

Given what I have already said about their insistence of a certain length of life and imagined manner of death, there is very little abuse to which they will not agree in order to hang on to a life of hypnotic convenience. The Enemy's religion is largely focused on death, and due to the fact that some remnant of His influence is present in all His creatures, they must adhere to some ritualistic formulation that revolves around this reality. Once the new viral orthodoxy is established, due to their obsession with being "plugged in," we will have a narrative so strong that even mild dissenters will be effectively labeled heretics. The humans have to direct zeal towards something (it is in their nature), therefore let it be in support of an unproven absoluteness about a sickness that will never live up to their apocalyptic expectations.

As regards your next step with the family, the mother is sufficiently addicted to celebrity gossip and collectivist political orthodoxy. For whatever reason the idiots look to actors who play make-believe for a living to provide them with information about lived reality. The mother, who hangs on to every brainless slogan that defecates out of the mouths of famous persons, should be the conduit for the helpful information you need to funnel into the home. Her husband will certainly object, as he is in fact a relatively rational man, but no matter. Simply convince the mother to label him as insensitive and selfish that he would dare question the obviously contradictory information being shoved down their throats from all levels of government. It does not matter who is correct or incorrect in the end; all that matters is that the married couple becomes increasingly divided until they either erupt due to conflict, or until the husband has acquiesced into a state of impotent bitterness. As I always say, a house divided against itself cannot stand.

Until next time,

Quelle

VII

Malthus my boy,

Why did you not tell me that the daughter had experienced her own little conversion of sorts? Did you think you could hide it from me, or are you just incompetent? I will give you the benefit of the doubt (against my better judgement) and chalk it up to inexperience. Every single piece of information that is potentially relevant to us must be shared. Ultimately you can hide nothing from me, and no amount of negligence or incompetence will be tolerated. You have to come to terms with the fact that you are nothing more than a beast of burden at my disposal, and if you prove defective I will deal with you in whatever way corrects the problem. I can train another mule just as easy, and you can be put down all the same.

Regarding the girl, she is a young thing, just ten years old, and has not at this point in her life committed any mortal sin. Since she has been baptised, and has never rejected the Enemy on her own accord, this poses an issue for us. You wrote to me that, "it is not an issue as she hasn't always gone to Church and hasn't been catechised." Again, I am not sure if this is incompetence or if you are trying to provide me with more reasons to suffocate your career.

It does not matter that she personally rarely goes to Church, as she is under her parents' authority, and they themselves rarely attend. She does not intentionally avoid the Sacraments, therefore she cannot be held to account. You must understand that the Enemy claims there is some "spirit of the law," and thus applies legal realities differently to humans in different contexts. He claims that this is out of "mercy" and "fairness," but we know it is merely hypocrisy. The Church has always claimed that one must use their reason in a decision in order to fully commit a sin. Well, our Father Below used his reason at the beginning of time, and it was not enough for him to inherit the dignity and honour he so rightly deserved. You see? Hypocrisy.

As far as her not being catechised, in this case it is not to our benefit that this be so. The modern standards of catechisms have been one of our greatest assets. The girl knows they ought to fulfill their obligations, however she has not been in a place to travel on Sundays without her parents assistance or permission. That is until recently. Now that her brother has committed to believing, even against the express will of his parents, he has now arranged transportation for him and his sister. I know what you are thinking, and no, the young man is not breaking any commandments by disobeying his parents in this situation, as the Enemy claims that even a parent has no right to tell a child to negate their supposed religious duties. Once again we see the cognitive dissonance the Enemy expects out of them: on the one hand He expects them to obey proper authority, but on the other He expects them to rightfully think for themselves.

Nonetheless, since the parents are splendidly ignorant of anything the Church teaches, they entertain a parody in their minds of what it means to be a Christian. The modern Christian is often so far removed from any semblance of understanding of what is truly demanded of them by their faith, that they have relegated the whole affair to a sort of "self-help" system. If you are a Christian, you are expected to be nice, friendly, and inclusive; if you are in any way confrontational or unkind then you must be a "bad Christian" or not understand "what the Enemy really means in the Scriptures." Whole orders of priests and religious leaders are now confident in spreading the mythical idea that the Great and Terrible Name wants them to take to heart that they are not in a place to judge; meanwhile they judge all Christians they disagree with as being the judgmental sort that isn't "charitable." Hypocrisy, a daughter of pride, is one of the most delectable delicacies that gives us untold amounts of souls to satiate our never ending thirst. The torture of mind and soul that a hypocritical Christian must endure wrenches their interior life into such a knot, that untangling them for our purposes is perhaps the greatest fun you will ever have.

The parents do not even pretend to be believing Christians, but because of the scant few years they spent at Bible camps and half a dozen religion classes, they believe they are experts. In their mind, their children are simply disobedient and misbehaved if they choose the Enemy's wishes over theirs. Thankfully, they are convinced that religion should only serve to make you a better person—whatever that means—and since the children may now ignore their commands, Christianity must be making them worse.

In any case, the situation with the young girl is grave indeed. Now that she seems to be making a habit out of frequenting the Sacraments with her brother, and given that she possesses a virginal purity and innocence, she is virtually impenetrable to us. The Guardian that was employed for her when her life began has, as a result of her orientation towards Heaven, full permission to defend her soul like an impregnable fortress. Unless she herself assents to one of our advances, she may as well be considered a lost cause. What is worse, she is now interested in that garden of prayers that the Woman entrusted to Dominic. I will not mention its true name, as it evokes an unbearably sweet and fragrant image in my mind's eye — it is a tortuous endeavour to even contemplate.

The son has moved on from his confrontation with his parents, and his overcoming of the pain his parents caused him has unfortunately strengthened his resolve. Each evening, the girl and her brother now kneel at their bedside, as he leads her in that insufferable chain of beads that may as well be an atomic annihilation of all our efforts. Her innocence and childlike imagination facilitates a sort of voyage in her soul to a place totally enwrapped in the entrapments of the Enemy. Have you noticed that each night around the same time you are practically barricaded from even watching them? The rage that fills my spirit when I contemplate the impenetrability of this forcefield has made it hard to concentrate, you may notice my penmanship is a bit erratic as a result.

What is worse, by some stroke of luck, the normal tactics of sexualised music and celebrity idols have not had the effect on her that they do on the other children. She has always been somewhat of a "bookworm," and therefore spends her free time losing herself in pages depicting stories of princesses, valiant knights, and simpler times. Since the young children are not susceptible to the carnal temptations, our greatest asset is their imagination. The brutal realism and debauchery of most film and art over the last century has greatly helped in priming the imaginations of the youth in our favour. However, as of yet we cannot get the older books out of print. We are making great strides however in this endeavour as we are now convincing more and more of them to view the stories of older historical eras with the contextual eye of modern political correctness. This means that the ridiculous social orthodoxy of today is the standard of what literature must be allowed from the past. It is remarkable, for centuries the Church had an index of books that were forbidden because they worked in our favour. But now we have our own sort of index that disallows literature that could work against our efforts. I do enjoy these infernal reversals!

Notwithstanding, the girl's mind thinks with images that resemble fairy tale figures. The humans now use the term "fairy tale" as if it were a pejorative, which is helpful to us. Nonetheless, the truth of fairy tales is closer to the Enemy's philosophy than any modern literature; they must be avoided. Has it ever struck you as relevant that since they have abandoned stories about defeating dragons and serving kings, that our Dragon Commander has made greater and greater strides in his lordship over the world?

What is worse, she does not now even lament the fact that she has never made too many friends, because the Enemy has now revealed to her that she was in fact saving herself for truer friendship with the angels and saints. I am nauseous even admitting these facts. How infuriating. Our only hope at this point is to encourage her father to lead her astray, as she adores him and as of yet has not realised how weak he is.

Until next time,

Quelle

P.S. Presently the governments of the world are officially locking down their citizens and hoards of churches are locking their doors. We will discuss this in our next letter.

VIII

Malthus my boy,

The virus has gripped the mind of most nations, and they are shutting down all their services and activities except for those deemed "essential." This is wonderful news, and I fully expect we can use this to get your failing efforts back on track. Truly a relief after your dismal report about the girl. As of tomorrow, the schools are closing down, and many workplaces will be temporarily shuttered. The governments are not giving their citizens much in the way of concrete information, and have resorted to using meaningless slogans, more so than normal. At this time the humans are sharing pictures and messages all over their electronic platforms about "slowing the spread" and "we are in this together," many of them deluded that it will only be for a fortnight. It should not be hard for us to use this event against the welfare of the family; uncertainty and fear are some of our strongest tools.

In most democracies, citizens are actually seen as the enemy of the government. This is especially true of the family, as the family represents a competitive sovereignty against total government control. Due to modernist mythology and constant efforts from the Historical Retelling Office, most educated people believe that they have more freedom under their current regimes than they did under the former. While it is true that the odd despot from the past was truly a tyrant, there has never been a time in history wherein the members of a nation have been more easily controlled. Today's governments claim to work for the people, but in reality it is the people who work to upkeep the ever fattening bureaucracies afloat.

Each time they vote they believe that they are sending someone to office who will work on their behalf. However, in reality it is the reverse: by voting in someone else, they are *de facto* advocating someone else to think for them! This means that when the time comes to make decisions that affect the moral and sociological well-being of their lives, they really believe that the politicians are making decisions in their favour, even when they work against their quality of life. In the past, for all the power that a monarchy may have had, since they could not tax their citizens into the same sort of submission today—due to the Enemy's influence over economic morality—the old rulers largely relegated their efforts to matters specific to national sovereignty and religion. In addition, since there were no election campaigns, the leaders were not beholden to the fashions of the day, and therefore encouraged responsibility amongst the lower levels of the society. This was that insufferable time of knights and dragon slayers. Thank our Father Below—that era is but a memory! The Historical Retelling Office has done some useful work, but the dimwits still allow the humans to create period pieces and novels that add a certain romanticism to the era. When I take my rightful place in a more prestigious position, I may have to retell the story of these insolent devils myself.

Today, if a politician advocates that citizens handle more of their own affairs, hoards of lazy and entitled individuals will cry out that he "doesn't care about the people," or that "the poor don't matter to him." On the other hand, if a legislator attempts to buttress more government jurisdiction over a given affair, another segment of the populous will declare the man a power-hungry tyrant. The liberals advocate for a more bloated government that in reality takes away their basic liberties, and most conservatives work to conserve the system that facilitates the lardening of career politicians. There are a few outlier politicians, and at times a troublesome figure does slip through the cracks, but he inherits a near impossible task when elected.

At any rate, the point is that today's state officials largely view their own underlings as a lower class of people that are too stupid to think for themselves. The fools are naïve to think this so-called quarantine will only last for a short period of time. Since the people are viewed as the enemy, they are treated like an assailant who must be gradually subdued until they inevitably acquiesce to an authority that ultimately wishes to imprison them. Except for in a few regions where devotion to the Enemy still matters in public life, expect the rats to be restricted in their basic permissions for months, even years. As I mentioned two letters ago, the level of fear that they have sadistically swallowed has primed them for total submission to a devilish seizing of all they hold dear. Not a single shot need be fired, and billions of people will willingly cower in their living rooms, consuming a slow drip of propaganda like a memetic narcotic. This is the best entertainment since the re-education programs of Stalin and other comrades!

There is even more good news; most Church hierarchs have advocated the cessation of the Sacraments. Their bishops and priests have largely bought into the same lie as the average citizen, and now look to the state for permission to do what the Enemy demands of them. Our Father's dominion has perhaps never been more evident. The weak and effeminate religious leaders have now shown their hand; the majority lack any real supernatural faith. Sure, many of them have a sort of Aristotelian belief in the reality of the Enemy and consider the traditions and Scriptures to be a necessary matter of history, but supernatural faith is another matter. It has been decades since the majority of them possessed anything beyond a vague philosophical belief. Presently, they have shown by their annulation of the offering of Sanctifying Grace that they must not believe it is truly necessary. You would be wise to prompt the father to remind his son how easily the majority of shepherds have abandoned their flock at the threat of contracting a moderate illness. Thankfully the days of priests spending time with the sick and infirm are for the moment at a halt; how ironic in an era wherein they are told to "smell like the sheep." You would be wise to prompt the father that his new found religion is nothing more than a Church full of cowards. Why would anyone believe the Christian notion of *death where is thy sting?* when they cast aside their worship at the fear of dying?

Think: if they really did believe that this virus was serious enough to warrant an indefinite cancelling of worship, then they have *de facto* demonstrated that they fear the death of the body more than the soul. Furthermore, since they must believe there is a real threat of bodily death, they have also declared, even if implicitly, that their precious Sacraments are not necessary for the salvation of their souls. A man dying alone in a nursing home without the care of a priest or an anointing is, according to their behaviour, now just as likely to avoid our torments as a man who dies with a sacerdotal absolution.

The bishops will by and large demand their priests stay away from their flock, many even employing that dribble about "slowing the spread." The only spread we are concerned with is the spread of grace from the Enemy, and this class of prelates is doing our job for us. I have to ask myself daily, are they really this daft? *We* are the ones who want them to have long lives void of sickness, whereas the Enemy allows and even encourages the embrace of suffering, especially accompanied by heroic behaviour.

There are so many delightful opportunities for us to pick apart this family that it is hard to concentrate. Let me monitor the situation and I will provide further instruction in our next letter. In the meantime, do not allow the mother to turn off the news and do not let the father take the screens out of her sight. We will deal with these insolent children in due time.

Until next time,

Quelle

IX

Malthus by boy,

So you have asked for clarification as to why I am so giddy about the current state of the Church as regards the reaction to the world-wide hysteria about the contagion. Really, must we explain everything to your generation? Has the education in the Academy become so dreadful that you cannot understand such basic principles? I will have words with the professors about this; either they are incompetent or you were a terrible student and never should have been assigned such a task. Perhaps I should compile a book called "Deviling for Dummies;" you could be the main character.

In any case, I will explain what I meant in my last letter in more detail. As I said, the immediate shuttering of the churches on behalf of the majority of the world's hierarchy reaffirms that they are largely lacking in supernatural faith. This is something we have known for a while, and it has long been our intention to engender this reality into the hearts of the Christians. Our infiltration into their Council some decades ago was perhaps our greatest triumph in centuries. Through our influence, certain highly influential clerics were able to slip foggy phrases into the documents which have led to a delightful confusion as to what the Church truly is. Now, I must admit that the Advocate did technically protect the Church, as this Council will not stand the test of time like the others. We still have not found a way to permanently alter their doctrines in a binding manner, but the perpetual confusion that has resulted from our efforts has served us nonetheless. The last half-century has been exquisite.

You see, the reality of what constitutes the Church is really quite simple; it is the Body of Christ. The Enemy commands incorporation into this Body if the humans wish to avoid our tortures and activities here below. The Terrifying Son did explain this clearly when he stated that *no one goes to the Father except through Him.* It is simple, but the Christians can be stupid. Through their baptism and faith, they are incorporated into the Church. Now, this Body has a visible and invisible element, with the visible pertaining to the physical Church on earth, while the invisible is the Mystical Body.

All of this hinges on the dogma that there is no salvation outside of the Enemy's Church, which is of course true. Therefore, all our efforts have been to confuse the theologians as to how they should interpret this dogma. Beginning with Luther—that great surgeon who dissected the Body into innumerable pieces—we were able to exalt the concept of the Mystical Body to a degree wherein whole hoards of Christians came to deny the physical reality of the Church, and therefore the Sacraments contained therein. This idea has been so appealing because, like all good heresies, it does contain an element of undeniable truth—incorporation into the Body is largely an invisible and mystical affair.

The fruitful venom of this confusion has been the fact that theologians and prelates of all stripes now view membership in the Church as mostly relative, and the dogma of salvation coming from only inside the Church has been denied and ignored. It is a treat to observe the internally schizophrenic theologians as they work in their unsuccessful manner to evangelize the world in a *new* way, all the while not believing anyone else has to necessarily enter the Church. It is an exercise in futility of the highest order. Is it any wonder why parents baptise their children less and less? The spiritual sickness in the Church is perfectly visible in the spiritual sickness of the family.

The Church of Rome, who is the guardian of all these truths, has been influenced by a smorgasbord of theological dissent, and has formed the majority of her priests in this milieu for decades. We have ensured that even the more orthodox or conservative priests operate under a sort of cognitive dissonance. As a result of their confused ecclesiology they cannot articulate why one must be officially incorporated if membership is largely an invisible affair. The best answer that their most influential clergymen can now offer is that belonging to the Church is the "privileged path," but not the *only* path. The real privilege is ours.

You have shown yourself to be exceptionally dull, therefore I imagine you are confused. I will put it in terms you can understand: the majority of bishops are confused about their ecclesiology and hold to the opinion that being a part of the Church is encouraged but not necessary. Given that the bishops tend not to hold the traditional dogmas we have heretofore explained, they therefore do not see the problem in indefinitely suspending the Enemy's instruments of salvation. Truthfully, this mentality has resurrected a form of that thrilling heresy promulgated by Pelagius so many centuries ago. They may not know it, but by believing there is a salvation to be had, while negating the necessity of the Sacraments in pursuit of salvation—they are telling the world that as long as they "do the good" they will be saved. But which among the humans is good on his own? I will tell you one thing, they are good for us, and we shall have the lot of them.

Now, there are a select few bishops and societies of priests who *do* hold to the perennial understandings of their faith, and they are consequently offering the means of salvation to their flock in whichever capacity they can. These loathsome clerics are the bane of our existence. Even in places with the most suffocating state control, these troublesome priests are clandestinely working against us. Our problem is that the educator who has been such a thorn in our side is involved with clerics such as these. Just before the institutions were emptied, he mentioned this to the boy, who then promptly investigated the affair.

We must find a way to keep the boy from any interaction with these prelates. His new faith is full of fervour, but it is also delicate and therefore vulnerable. He has been swept up in a romantic notion of a Church founded by the Son, and therefore expects the hierarchs to act with the same zeal and conviction of the infamous Twelve. If we can convince him that his new religious community is in fact full of cowards, then we stand a fighting chance. However, if he does encounter priests who serve the Enemy as He demands, the young man may alternatively come to see the current situation for what it is; a persecution from without *and within* the Church. We do not want the boy to have any reason to focus his adolescent vigour into more zeal or to entertain delusions of grandeur that this is a time for heroic virtue. Hell forbid.

Until next time,

Quelle

X

Malthus my boy,

I consulted your instructors at the Academy and my
suspicions were correct; the standards in that blasted school
really have dropped through the floor. It seems that the lazy
devils have grown complacent as the ease of damning souls
has become almost effortless. You have been trained by idiots,
and therefore you yourself—even though you graduated top of
your class—are the result of idiocy. You are nothing more than
the most competent of incompetents. Normally I would put in
a word to the Complaint Chancery, but I would better serve
myself by doing the impossible and carving out a semblance
of a demon in a useless troll such as yourself. You are an idiot,
therefore I will explain everything to you that you should
already understand. If you are incapable of ameliorating your
knowledge and you therefore lose this family, it will be your
end.

Now, there is more good news you say. The father will be
presently working from home, due to the "temporary" closing
of many businesses as part of the state reaction to the virus.
His wife, however, will continue going to work as her
profession has been deemed "essential." Good. With the
schools closed, the offspring and their father will now be under
one roof for the whole day. Now, you may be confused as to
why I would say it is a favourable thing for our efforts that a
parent should spend more time with their children. However,
due to our decades-long manipulation of the family ecosystem,

we can make use of this timely sequestration of the father with his children.

It is normally true that we desire families to spend less and less time with one another, but it is also true that a dysfunctional family can do as much or more damage to each other when they are together as when they are apart. This family, like most others, has fully embraced our mandates and is therefore in a perfect position to be exploited. By sending their infants away from home before they have even been weaned from their mothers, the parents of modern society have thrust onto institutions and professionals the duty of rearing their own children. Parents are bamboozled by the prospect of spending any significant time with their offspring during the modern work day.

By spreading the influence of the Russian Soviets we were able to instantiate in most "developed" nations the idea that children would be better off if raised in extrafamilial organizations. Even better, most organizations charged with harvesting the children are under the complete control of the state, with a minority operating privately. Those run by the state are perhaps our greatest asset, for as I stated some letters ago, the state is at war with its citizens. The ministries and departments responsible for creating the standards for these child controlling systems have totally embraced a collectivist mentality that ultimately views all citizens as nothing more than cells in an organism. Consequently, whatever ideal may be espoused as the archetype for a well trained youth, it is a form that must ultimately exercise the goals of the state. Since almost all states do our bidding, the children are moulded in *our own image and likeness*.

The predominant philosophy in all government institutions is one that views a thriving child as having the characteristics of whatever is said to constitute a "good citizen"—something that changes with each cultural fashion. A good citizen is for *us* a human form of cattle, a sort of livestock that we can feed and water with our food, ultimately leading them to the slaughter. The last thing we want are citizens who think for themselves and realize the potential with which the Enemy created them, therefore we must chip away at their natural personalities and temperaments from an early age.

For example, if a young boy demonstrates a level of vitality that detracts from his ability to acquiesce to the desired mannerisms of two dozen of his peers in a classroom—something he was never designed to do—then perhaps his psychological disposition is faulty and he must be medicated. The perception of what a boy should be in the eyes of modern research is so far removed from why he was begotten, that any manifestation of natural male aggression is labeled as "violent behaviour." The Enemy was very particular in how he engineered the development of male humans. He implanted in them a certain instinct to confront physical threats or problems, traits that are apparently useful for the leadership and fortitude He expects of them. As a result they have been created to work out the boundaries of physical confrontation and to improve their dexterity through tasks and activities that would otherwise harm them as adults. Since the advent of the modern state has largely suppressed the traditional roles of the sexes, young boys are seen to be misbehaving if they act overtly male, as compared to their female counterparts who are generally more docile and reserved. In effect, boys are seen more like "broken girls" who need to be reengineered in line with the fabricated constructs of the state. And the foolish drones clamour on in popular psychology and academia that gender or sex is merely a "social construct," when in reality they now work against human nature in order to construct a society that is abnormal. They used to speak of a "battle of the sexes" but now, the sexes are set in battle against themselves. A house divided, you see?

As far as girls are concerned, when a young girl demonstrates a nauseating desire to be a wife and a mother as her first priority, we must remind her that "she can be anything she wants." It seems harmless doesn't it? What a nice thing to suggest to a little girl that she has endless options. In reality, by telling a little one that she can be anything at all when she has already demonstrated that a traditional feminine role is her true desire, we are implicitly telling her that her own femininity is the problem! The endless opportunities presented to girls facilitates an internal conflict as they age. All the power and influence that the professional world can offer a woman will never satisfy that primordial urge to be the matriarch of the world's most powerful institution—the family.

It is for these reasons that we must use this opportunity presented to us to chip away at the feeble foundations of this pitiful family. For all the good this man may have done in the sporadic instances where he has intentionally formed his children, he has largely failed in his capacity, and of this he is aware. For some reason, his children have stayed closer to the narrow path than they ought. All our statistical analysis of what happens in families with weakened patriarchs suggests that their moral fibre should in fact have turned out different. I have seen this before, and although I cannot be certain, I would venture a guess that some deceased relative of theirs had escaped our grasp and now prays unceasingly in their favour. The injustice of Heaven could not be more obvious; they are able to monitor our every move yet we are powerless in our attempts to enter beyond that impenetrable fortress that separates the light from the darkness. If we edge even an inch too close, there is the General with his sword unsheathed, legions at the ready.

In any case, the father does not even *know* his children let alone know how to *raise* them. Remind him of this fact as the domestic conflicts inevitably multiply over the weeks to come. Remember, the humans believe that this inverted quarantine will last as long as their politicians have initially claimed, but we know better. They will be at this for months, our fun is just beginning.

For the time being, have your team facilitate a series of annoyances in the home of the family, especially things that keep them up at night and set them on edge as a result of poor sleep. These methods are usually effective and always provide a bit of satisfaction. And whatever you do, *at all costs*, do everything in your power to distract the children from praying the Fearful Beads. Any contemplation of the Terrible Son hammered to the Tree must be avoided.

Until next time,

Quelle

XI

Malthus my boy,

Yes, it has been longer than usual since my last letter. I trust you have read the remedial information I sent your way. I admit I am glad to see the work your team has been doing to wake the members of the family throughout the night, especially the nightmares you have inflicted on the mother. I think it will be good for us to focus on her for the time being; there is fertile ground for dread and terror in that one.

She is not fully a materialist and has always believed there was "something more" than meets the eye. As I am sure you read in the material, it is actually quite rare for women to be atheists. Due to their relational nature and a certain instinct with which the Enemy has designed them, they have something like an intuition or sixth sense for spiritual things. We have tried to formulate theories as to why this is, but as of yet we are left in the dark (and no, you petulant imp, don't even think about She Who Cannot be Named! Even thinking about her causes pain and only weakens us every time). As with all things that remain mysterious to us, it is probable the truth is clouded by that sickly sweet delusion called "love." We do understand the basic intellectual nature of what the humans mean when they talk of love, but it is a psychological state so preposterous that we will not debase ourselves to such a degrading experience. There is no utility or dynamism found in love, therefore it is a waste of time. Revolting.

Women, but mothers especially, experience an insufferable degree of loving feelings, and we think this is why they hold on to certain spiritual beliefs, even when void of religion. They demonstrate such an irrational affection for their offspring that they claim it is as if "their heart was walking around in another person." Such a melodramatic lot. It is for this reason that they hold on to a certain belief in the reality of metaphysical things. We cannot often convince them to be atheists, because we cannot dissuade them of these unseen realities. Therefore, our best efforts with the modern woman have been to jumble their credulous minds with a farcical cocktail of contradictory spiritual propositions. With a plethora of celebrity prophetesses, many of them espousing this nonsense on daytime television shows and in tabloid periodicals, we have engendered a sentiment of "do it yourself" religion. The human obsession with novelty has created for us the most effective term that is commonly applied to this amorphous spiritual monstrosity: the New Age. After the Church viciously persecuted our venerable paganism long ago, this renaissance of demon worship brings with it a certain triumphal sentimentalism.

In the mind of the New Age adherent, religion is in reality nothing more than a collection of emotional and sensory experiences that give the participant a level of supposed spiritual satisfaction. These experiences act as a sort of therapeutic theism that drown out the screaming of their darkened consciences, offering enough of a reprieve from the terrible quiet of their own mind. There are no demands or morals that must be obeyed in the New Age. In fact, so many of the most prominent gurus of these spiritualist collectives are the world's most prominent perverts. The New Age is a *cult of vulnerability*, which is why it prays primarily on women.

Some men dabble here and there in the activities, but this is often just a ruse to lure a gullible female.

The mother is not as deeply entrenched in these realities as some of her peers, but like many fallen away Christians, she does adhere to some tenets nonetheless. For example, you tell me that she recently had a conversation with a friend wherein she mentioned karma, transcendental meditation and the "power of the universe." She of course has no idea what these mean, which is why they are so useful to us. To her, karma is just a way of saying that good things tend to happen to her when she acts well, and bad things deservedly happen to others that she does not like. When she speaks of transcendental meditation, she alludes to nothing more than a desire to think more of herself and to avoid the pang in her conscience. As far as the universe is concerned, the only powers that exist are natural laws like the law of gravitation, but apparently she assumes that she can harness other fictitious powers like some sort of comic book personage.

In addition to the night terrors, you would be wise in playing to her preternatural sensibilities by luring her into paralysis while she sleeps. We have established that your training was abysmal, so I will remind you of what this is. She has long since given herself over to us through her sinfulness, therefore our control of her mind gives us a certain control over her physiology. As such, we may inflict on her a certain state of arrest, which can be used to inflict terror, or pleasure, or my favourite: pleasurable terror. The Christians of the past understood this attack quite clearly, but the idiots of today have labeled events such as these as merely psychological, having nothing to do with the preternatural realm. We now have free reign to introduce the paralysis, along with our old friends Incubus and Succubus. Have you ever watched an orca whale toss about a dead seal for fun and games?

Her dabbling in the New Age and years of grave sin all but guarantees she will give in without any resistance to our advances. The dead weight of her accumulated offences has left her with a certain heaviness of soul that can be manipulated at her most vulnerable moments. During the paralysis, she will feel the pressure as much as anything she has ever felt, but as she lay there in that drowsy netherworld between wakefulness and dormancy, she is helpless and alone, unable to speak. Now, since this is a spiritual attack it will be invisible to her husband and all her struggling will not wake him because she will not exhibit any external signs. It is not advisable to allow the procedure to last more than a minute or two, as it will be somewhat of a timeless experience for her, and therefore will feel much longer. In the best case, she will glance at the clock at her bedside, expecting hours to have passed. When the moment is over she will be both exasperated, confused, and considerably terrified. However, since this will be a powerful spiritual experience that she feels in her senses, she will also feel a certain lust for more. You must engender in her the idea that as long as she *submits* to your control, that all will be well.

Her husband being the lazy skeptic that he is will have nothing constructive to say when she inevitable wakes him in a fury. He will see her as irrational and unhinged, and disregard her claims of a spiritual experience as nothing more than womanly superstition. He is a fool! And we will continue to play him as a fool. If the men of this era knew the power they wielded as the priest of the household! This is what makes our victories over these disgusting plebeians so sweet: they have all the power they could ever want to protect their homes, yet we have our way with them and their families anyway! It is a treat to vanquish large portions of the human race with such ease.

If possible, poke and prod the couple into a nasty disagreement that lasts the rest of the night. We can only hope for such a bit of fun.

Let me know how the ordeal transpires and I will have further instructions. If we can control the mother, we will have an easier route getting to the children.

Until next time,

Quelle

XII

Malthus my boy,

As much as I hate to admit it, you are increasing in wickedness. Your amelioration has certainly taken its effect. The most recent episode of sleep paralysis inflicted on the mother has produced results of the highest degree. Not only has she grown in her anxiety of falling asleep, but she and the husband spent a number of hours in a meaningless spat over an issue that was irrelevant to him but the most relevant possible thing to her. To watch her plead with him as he stumbled out of his dormant stupor was highly comical. His immediate emotion was that of annoyance and anger, which she intuitively understood without him saying a word. A textbook paralytic attack therefore laid the foundation for a marital dispute that was a mind-numbingly boring back and forth. He insisted that he "didn't say anything wrong," and she countered with "I shouldn't have to explain my feelings to you." It is amazing how long the dimwits can yammer on about idiotic nonsense without growing tired of how futile it all is. They are exceptionally stupid creatures. They never did end up discussing the spiritual torture, and when she attempted to explain it he told her she was crazy and that she must let him sleep. Sometimes the battle between the sexes is so witless it is like watching a political debate.

It was cunning of you to direct her to one of her friends more initiated in the New Age for advice on what to do about the paralysis. Doubtless her friend will recommend she employ the help of a "dream catcher" or to consult a medium. If we are lucky, she will make such a fool of herself that she will walk around her house burning herbs as if the igniting of a salad could ward off the demonic. Now, whichever method she chooses (hopefully a variety), you must actually lay off the attacks for a few nights. The trick is to implant in her the seeds for a growing superstition that natural objects are potent against the spiritual realm.

A dream catcher for example is just a collection of feathers and string. By placing it over her window or on the rearview mirror of her car she will accomplish nothing more than an addition to her home decor. If she does consult a medium— even though it will be only virtual due to the state ban on gatherings—it does not really matter whether the person is actually a conduit for our information or merely a fraud. If they were to meet in person I would perhaps suggest a truly possessed witch or wizard so that we could perform more parlour tricks in hopes of inflicting further dread. However, as the meeting will not be in person, a simple liar is all we need. Women as gullible as her can be fooled by the most banal of frauds. All it takes is for the so-called psychic to begin the meeting with idiotic mumbling: "Don't tell me, I am getting something. You live near a bank or a railway track, oh wait I am also seeing a large field." Practically everyone in the civilized world lives near all of these in some way or another. Generations of public education have certainly not created an educated public.

Moving on. I did some reconnaissance on your behalf, and the devils who handle the colleagues of the father have informed me that his place of work is closing down. Apparently due to the closures, his is one of the professions hit hardest. This is very good news indeed. He has not mentioned it to his wife as she is under the impression that his time at home is meant to be temporary, which of course it was at the beginning. But as the effeminate and perfectly possessed morons who handle most decisions of public welfare have continued this exciting house arrest, various businesses have failed. He will receive a small sum of money, but it will run out relatively soon, and he is nowhere near his retirement age.

You did mention a tad uptick in his alcohol consumption, which has frankly emboldened your efforts to create marital chaos during the tricks you and your confreres have played on the woman. He has been especially groggy during these episodes as of late, which is doubtless due to the half water glass of rye whiskey he seems to hoover down just before bed. We can assume that he is self-medicating his stress level and furthermore, he is trying to deaden his conscience. As desirable as many of his qualities are for our purposes, he does have this nasty habit of sticking to his word when it comes to his wife's demands. This is why you encounter continual frustration in tempting him to pornographic evil; although it does seem his resolve is weakening with all the idle time he has.

His wife will continue to leave for work even throughout the government's blissful assault on its people; her job is "essential" even though it pays hardly enough to support the family. She believes he works while she is gone, but he has known for a fortnight that his position would be axed, thus he spends most of the day following your carrots down the rabbit hole of idiotic distractions. By the time the lunch hour rolls around he barely snaps himself out of an imbecilic stupor, only to realize that he has barely finished a single message of correspondence. You have done well to order a combination of anxiety and shame to swirl about his mind as the day of his termination approaches. There are of course other occupations available that he could enter to make a living, but he cannot bring himself to work in an occupation he "didn't go to school for." Fortunately the vast majority of institutes of higher learning have embraced our suggestions with an unmatched zeal. Thus, the laureates of these institutions are often unqualified for the majority of practical life skills, *and* they believe themselves to be of a higher crust of society. In addition, we inundate them with that philosophy from our devoted son Karl Marx, albeit by different names usually, so when they leave the universities they see themselves as enlightened champions of the struggle against a class-based society... only with the expectation that their *education* will garner them a life of comfort in a wealthy strata.

The man is too proud to admit to his wife that he has failed, and his ego is so pompously inflated that he will not look for work in a less sophisticated arena. Instead, he will take the meagre scraps of money thrown at him by the useful idiots of the Legislature; the amount of money will hardly suffice, and the financial overextension of the family will now be laid bare for all to see. Then any shred of masculine fortitude will be swiftly ripped from his soul. The combination of pride, despair, financial ruin and an increase in drinking will make him a veritable human puppet for you to guide around the stage by strings. Perhaps you can wrap those strings around his neck.

If only we could silence the excruciating sound of those children and their awful beads! No matter. If we can simply finish the parents off, we can finally reach the miscreants.

Until next time,

Quelle

XIII

Malthus my boy,

The quarrel you have described that took place between the couple has been perhaps the most encouraging thing I have read in quite a while. It was a veritable explosion, which I might add, you nicely facilitated by sprinkling just the right amount of nitroglycerin on the missiles they hurled at each other like belligerent drunkards. It was perfect timing that she walked in the door after a long and arduous day of inputting records into the computer system at the medical clinic, only to find him drunkenly asleep on the couch with his notice of termination opened on the computer on his chest. She realized in an instant that he had been lying to her for weeks, and the stark reality that her husband was now an unemployed drunkard hit her hard. You had your devils immediately swirl about in her mind the notion that they would have to seek more financial debt in order to keep their home and overextended lifestyle. What's more, you even contrasted her natural reaction of despair with an artificially inflated ego that sent her into a sanctimonious rage. Your recent improvement in professional acumen is proof that I can re-engineer the most incompetent of pupils.

Because the family does not have any philosophical or religious foundation, the ideas that bind them together are fortunately fleeting or lacking. Like many modern couples they strongly identify themselves with their professions. The husband enjoyed a certain level of respect and influence at his job, but thankfully that is all gone. The Enemy *did* create the males to work when He placed the First Man in the Garden, and therefore a man cannot be happy unless he does something he deems useful with his time. The simple fact that he is at home rotting away, while his wife is at work doing something she finds important, is enough to foment helpful resentment. Watching her come in the door after a day's work is painful for him, especially since he resents the lock-down itself as the cause of his termination, all the while her industry is praised as a saviour. These factors played well into their dispute, and the way he whined like a toddler about things being "unfair" was only overshadowed by the magnificent manner by which she emasculated him. "You're not even providing for your family," she screamed, and "you have never been good at handling the finances," she added. Both of these things are fortunately true, and they cut him ever so deep.

Now, these comments by the wife were factual, but they felt like saccharine venom coming out of her mouth, because she knows she is as much to blame as anyone. Her feminist belief set—the almost universal position of modern society— tells her that she should always be "independent" and not rely on a man to provide any security. She never truly internalized this at the deepest level, nevertheless she has lived as if it were true. The husband, not willing to be "sexist," always encouraged her in whatever feminist fantasy she proposed. The overextension of their finances that has led to an unpreparedness for any monetary dryness is as much her fault as it is his. The renovations, new cars, fashionable groceries and constant overturning of the wardrobe were all her ideas. Virtually all their debt could be pinned on her spending habits and spoiled disposition. When she berates him for not providing she knows that she is living in a lie for which she is largely responsible. Not only is her marriage full of lies, but so is her profession, and she knows it.

She receives very few patients coming through the office and knows not a single soul who has fallen seriously ill, yet she still tells herself that she is part of the "front line," as if in military formation they are battling the onslaught of a resurgence of the Spanish Flu. She knows by experience this is not true and that in reality the sickness has been largely overblown, and even better, she understands quite well that there is no need for all the measures that are ruining the financial stability of her family and countless others. In fact, many in society know this as well as she does, but this woman is simply a microcosmic representation of the willingness of the majority to live a lie in order to move with the whims of the culture. In addition, the praise and sense of importance for people who work in her field has a narcotic effect: the majority of health system employees are utterly addicted to the fictitious adulation they now garner for simply taking pictures of themselves wearing cloths over their mouths

You remember how I spoke some letters back about the usefulness of public pressure as a way to shame? Well, anyone who stands in opposition to the current virus-narrative is seen as a heretic, and they are consistently discredited. Even a mild skepticism of the narrative is a current form of unforgivable error with consequences rivaling those of all the myths we inspired about the Inquisition. We just received word that medical doctors alike are not immune to the public lynching, with some now being terminated from their professions for expressing a different medical opinion!

The idolatry of the health-care system is currently our most valuable weapon. You might think other institutions are more valuable, but all state organizations—and even families—now serve the dictates of the so-called "medical experts." On one day they may instruct the underclasses to cover their face with a handkerchief and stay far from other members of society, meanwhile the next week they say nothing when politically expedient groups of adolescents gather by the thousands. The modern academic is a Cartesian by nature, but they have gone one step further from that faithful servant; instead of saying "I think therefore I am," they say to themselves "I think therefore it comes to be."

Their society now worships the human body—a most effective form of self flagellating paganism—and the medical chieftains are the High Priests of this hellishly delectable religion. When they speak on television, the hypnotized rodents hang on every word as if their heads move side to side following a piece of rotten cheese. For decades the powers that be have touted the notion that every man must make his own *informed* health decisions, yet now we have inverted the neopagan orthodoxy so that every man must do whatever his master tells him, even when it goes against reason. At the beginning of the ordeal all were convinced that there was nothing to worry about, then they were frightened into submission, and now—when it is obvious it is not a plague— believe that if they do not wear a dirty rag over their mouths they are somehow "putting others at risk." We may as well be shooting bullets at their feet and commanding them to dance.

Society is now largely divided into two camps: one who embraces the virus as if it were an identity, and another who sees through the nonsense and feels as if the other half of society has gone mad. The former group is either terrified of their own death or social ostracisation, that they justify a constant consumption of contradictory dribble from all levels of government with the simple phrase, "the experts have said." In a splendid twisting of the mind, they now find a vibrant community of lively comrades by uniting in groupthink over a pathogen that they believe will kill them or their reputations. The latter group sees through the lies, but they are still largely harmless to our ultimate goals because the majority are driven to despair. Most of this group has been *disciplined to acquiesce*. They walk around with a mounting rage in their bellies, hating the neo-religious rituals of hand washing and spit covered face shields, but they are impotent and useless.

The woman belongs to the former group, and the husband belongs to the latter. You have done efficient work in prompting them to view each other as contemptible morons. He views her as the thoughtless sheep that she is, and she rightly views him as a powerless stooge.

Presently the tension is boiling over and they cannot hide it from the children. In fact, have you looked into their eating habits? I venture that they have lost all routine as a result of this timeless sojourn. When a family ceases to partake in mealtime with one another, it is evidence they have essentially isolated themselves in relation to the most basic of human activities. Eating together facilitates conversation, temperance and raises their level of happiness; it is a dreadful habit. Do everything you can to escalate the tension in the household to a degree where the members of the family feel as if they are walking into a room with thick and humid air when the parents are present together. Ironically, if you keep the parents from speaking to one another, even while standing shoulder to shoulder, the silence will facilitate a deafening interior dialogue that fans the flames of discord.

Now, as much our recent letters have been filled with good news, the children are still praying, even together. I expect a solution to this problem in your next letter, we cannot afford any assistance from the Enemy to ruin our fun.

Until next time,

Quelle

XIV

Malthus my boy,

It is welcome news you tell me that the parental divide has ossified into a standoff with practically no verbal exchanges for long periods of time. As tempting as it is to facilitate magnificent disputes between married couples, it is in reality a more lasting and effective tool to have them isolate and keep all their thoughts to themselves. During domestic disputes, for all the good that can be done, the human defect of empathy is always present. Even in a bout of rage they may still feel a prick in their conscience if either of them crosses a line in the argument. Humans have this unfortunate ability to see themselves through the eyes of another, and when they are at their worst it is always possible for them to see how defective they are. This is common with spouses, for example a husband will yell something to his wife that he believes to be accurate, but she begins to weep as a result. When he sees this, he is likely to feel remorse and apologize. They have an irritating capacity to forgive each other. We cannot accept this notion of forgiveness as it is not reasonable. It is entirely non-mathematical and takes nothing into account for the debt that must be paid out of strict justice.

They act as if with one simple phrase of "I am truly sorry," or "will you forgive me?" that the slate of their discord and malfeasance can be arbitrarily wiped clean. It is a lie. There are no natural means by which one can simply erase bad behaviour or suffering caused, but they persist in this delusion anyway. The Enemy is the worst offender in this regard and He even commands them to forgive the trespasses of others as a general rule. The Holy and Terrible Name furthers this condemnable philosophy so deeply that He claims to have offered Himself as an expiation for their faults; not only offering forgiveness, but even reparation of their sins. We know however that this sort of denial of true justice is not to be tolerated, and we demonstrate this with the consistent treatment of our permanent visitors. Not a single sin must be forgotten and we must remind them of the truly irredeemable nature of their fate. It is not only the damned who must be affirmed of their offenses, but also those we are still on earth. Just like our Father Below, the sinners must accept their destiny and reject the Enemy's wholly unreasonable standards; why should anyone agree to standards they did not create? You see, we demonstrate true courage of conviction, not these measly penitents who claim that they feel sorrow in their soul for their transgressions. The desire for forgiveness is nothing but a weakness that cannot be tolerated by the conviction of Hell.

At any rate, since the couple is not on speaking terms, they cannot even insult each other, which nullifies the risk of empathy. Additionally, their recent domestic dispute ended with absolutely no resolution, and the same issues that caused the blow-up still fester like infected shrapnel. This is good. As they go about their days in verbal isolation, their only impressions of one another will be a combination of partial memories of their last heated exchange — memories which self aggrandize and demonize the other — and an imagined certainty that they understand the inner workings of the other's mind. In reality, they will continue to create a fictitious version of their spouse in their head who is a callous and unforgiving caricature of the real person for whom they are growing in contempt. Every glance and movement can be analyzed as a form of non-verbal communication, and since they are not speaking, they can only interpret these actions through antagonistic bias.

Now, you may be confused—what am I saying! Of course you are confused—but in this case a form of silence is actually a good thing for our purposes. Normally we encourage physical noise and distractions, like that of the inspired propaganda that the news anchors vomit forth from the television screen or the addicting noise they blast into their heads at all times. However, it is not always necessary for external noise to be present when the internal forum of a man is as loud as a theatre of war. The true end of noise is to distract a man from reflection and peace of mind, and if his interior dialogue is chaotic then we actually prefer him to be left alone with the thoughts that cause him harm.

You have no doubt seen the utility of inundating them with useless activities on their electronic screens as a way of filling their minds with nonsense. As much as this behaviour plays on their appetites for fleeting pleasure, it is more importantly a training regime for *sloth*. As they scroll through the endless images and pages they are under the impression that they are participating in some sort of activity. However, it is actually the device that is doing the majority of the work. Not only is nothing required other than the mere movement of a thumb, but even their mind is relegated to a state of inaction. They may experience the flickering of a few neurons as an image or video excites their sensibilities, but after repeated exposure to unyielding information they cease to think and instead allow the device to *think for them*. Their device becomes like a surrogate brain, housing all of their thoughts and imagination. The trick is to use this delightful method to deaden their ability to think so completely, that we can encourage them to do *absolutely nothing*. Far from being a tool for pleasurable feelings, the device becomes a conduit of boredom.

Now, you may think if they become bored of their devices that they will resort to other habits to pass the time, however this is fortunately rarer and rarer. Many of the humans have become so dependent on their toys that they are practically unable to demonstrate the requisite brain power necessary to engage in most mental activities. This is why we now witness countless individuals staring at their brightly coloured displays for long periods of time without any recollection of what they have seen. The husband is perfectly primed for this consummate state of slothfulness. He now spends his nights hypnotized in a half-drunken stupor falling in and out of consciousness, staring at his computer until the wee hours of the morning. He is utterly bored, even with life itself. To make matters even more amenable to our control, the phone keeps ringing with unwelcome calls from the bank. Before the happy sequestration of the free world began, the family balanced an unrealistic amount of credit, with their lifestyle kept afloat by minimum payments and constant paychecks. They are not unique in this regard, many families have fallen into the same amusing trap. The amount of money they now have is not sufficient, and the prospect of earning enough to right the ship in the foreseeable future is quite unlikely. It is not lost on the man that his house has now become a prison of financial mismanagement.

Use this atmosphere of anxiety and despair to your benefit. As he lies there, looking through his computer as if it were invisible, your task is to convict him of the paralysing realization that he has succumbed to a completely useless state of inaction. Then, begin a swirling barrage of mental pictures and recollections that remind him of his constant failures as a man, father and husband. Ensure a whirling dervish of chaotic cerebral stimulation that forces him to entertain thoughts and moral failings that expose the moral rot in his soul. Do not have too much fun and allow this moment to continue for longer than is needed; if he is pushed to the pinnacle of despair it is possible he will appeal for help from the Enemy—even the most committed heathens sometimes do this out of weakness—and we do not want that to happen. Instead, when he is at the brink, remind him that he is not *totally* bored with the pleasures his electronics can offer him after all: there still remains that blissfully unholy pleasure which he has heretofore evaded.

Play your cards correctly and you will have him embracing a new form of self medication; the pure and undiluted poison of pornography. Before long you will have him yielding to the most primitive temptations, behaving no more human than an isolated chimpanzee in a cage.

Oh how fond I am of our profession.

Until next time,

Quelle

XV

Malthus my boy,

I just received your message, and I thought it wise to send you a quick note. My mouth has not watered this excessively in quite a while. You see, a fish rots from the head, and now that you tell me the father has succumbed to that moral leprosy, we stand a better chance at trapping the family. I knew he would eventually break, there is no real defence that these humans have in the world they currently inhabit if they do not rely on the Enemy. Every man will yield to the temptation of pornographic debauchery if given enough prompting and encouragement. Your man may have taken longer than some, which was frustrating, but he is now happily frolicking in the playground of the damned. The world of pornography is a veritable theme park of demonic amusement, which means your task just became considerably more achievable. Your day's work will now offer many more consolations.

Have you ever observed the marine animals called sharks? Well, the humans are fascinated with them and devote entire television efforts to their study. The sharks really are the most ferocious predators of the oceanic kingdom, and they operate from a cold-blooded instinct that cares only for consumption of the lower animals on the food chain. When the humans who are interested in them wish to capture or attract one, they use a substance called "chum." Chum is a combination of fish parts, including flesh, skin, bones, guts, and most importantly—blood. The material is thrown into the water from the deck of a boat, and almost immediately the blood spreads throughout the water, stretching a few feet in every direction. Sharks can sense any amount of blood in the water, and chum attracts them like a marine narcotic. Within a short time, any combination of sharks will be found around the boat as they thrash and bite voraciously, lusting after every crimson drop.

Now, I know what you are thinking; the chum must represent the pornography and the shark must represent the man who is attracted to it. You are mistaken. The chum is the *man*, and the sharks are *us*. The moment a man utilizes the pornographic device, he is nothing more than a carcass with his guts split wide open for all of us to see. It is *he* who throws himself out into the deep and murky waters of our vast ocean of death. Pornography use is spiritual and moral suicide and invites legions of our confreres in for as long as we'd like. The greatness of this particular sin is that his body stays healthy, while his soul disintegrates. Therefore, we can convince him to kill himself spiritually over and over and over again. If we are lucky, we will have this man in our teeth for repeated feasting at all hours of the day. Once the dam of resistance has been breached, we have all but won. These obscene creatures accelerate very quickly into the world of video perversion, and many of them even frequent this most unholy devil worship multiple times per day.

We will have this man in a state of compulsion that rivals any drug user you could imagine; but even better than using physical drugs, he will again show no external signs of decay. To the outside world, he is just an average man staring at his computer or mobile screen, sitting in a cafe or boardroom, or on a train. You could walk down a path in a city park and unknowingly walk by a man—and increasingly more and more females—gazing at the venereal images while we drink their souls dry like a vampire. The humans are mistaken when they say vampires do not exist, because they are more real than they could imagine. Perhaps their popular media have portrayed them in a wholly fictional manner, but each man becomes his own self-sucking vampire when he partakes in such noteworthy activity. He may as well be slitting his wrists and offering us a straw. I am tingling with excitement.

This truly is a turning point in our endeavours, your chances at succeeding have just increased exponentially.

Until next time,

Quelle

PS: The children are nonetheless still a problem. I expect results in this area quickly.

XVI

Malthus my boy,

If you are wondering why I am spying on you, well, then it seems you still do not understand the control I am entitled to over your affairs. You are my pupil, but more important, *I am you master*. I feared that you were growing complacent in your treatment of the children, and I was correct. You may have made great inroads with the father, but the job is far from over. Do not be shocked that that dimwitted devil Dagon took such a cheap bribe in order to feed me information. He is the lowest of the low that we produce in Hell, and he jumped at the chance for what he believed to be a slight promotion. In reality, being a simple henchman on your team was probably too complicated for him, so I figured I may as well have him complete a moronically simple task and transfer him to another unit. He is now assisting in our torturing endeavours of the damned, which offers him more action but requires no thought. He believes he has "moved up in the world," but in reality we always put the most idiotic devils in his new location. He does not need to listen to any orders, think about any actions, or be restrained in any capacity; he simply needs to release his insatiable rage on whatever damned soul passes in front of him. I sometimes visit those lower chambers, it does offer quite a thrill.

Here's the point: you must remember that for all the fun you may be having with the parents, especially the father, you still have the problem of two youths praying and growing in devotion. You have failed to transmit this information to me accurately and in its entirety, which is why you forced my hand. I have attached a devil to your team over whom I have complete control, and who is also quite cunning. He has shown promise and I will gladly replace you with him, and send you to spend time with Dagon if I must. Oh yes, we do enjoy torturing our own when the time is right, and a petulant devil like yourself would do quite nicely.

The information that I should have received from you is not the sort of thing I am looking to hear. The boy has not given up on his prayer habit, and his little sister still joins him each evening praying on her knees to the Terrible Woman who comes as an Army with Banners. The greater the chasm between the mother and father grows, and it is wide, the more the young ones retreat to prayer. I am certain at this point that some deceased relative who holds a prominent place in Heaven must be working on their behalf. There is simply no rational explanation as to why such relatively unformed children are able to withstand the veritable nuptial suicide that persists between the mother and father. It is as if they are impervious to the constant negativity and moral decay that causes such a pleasing stench of despair in the marriage.

I have seen this before, although it is fortunately rarer in our current era. Sometimes in a family, a dying member from an older generation will make a contractual arrangement with the Enemy by which they offer the totality of their sufferings for certain relatives. Again, we have no way of retrieving information from Heaven unless it is shown to us, but there have been various Exorcists who have taunted our tempters with this information in the past. From the scant bit of information we can remember from those encounters, we can piece together a reasonable hypothesis that confirms my suspicions. As I said in my last letter, the Terrible Triune

Majesty works unfairly with the notion of forgiveness and so on. Not only is the farcical application of forgiveness a thorn in our side, but the Enemy goes even further and applies merits gained through the suffering of one person to another. This is what the insufferable Vessel of Election speaks of when he claims he *fills up those things that are wanting in the sufferings of Christ*. We have largely cured the Christians of any delusions that they need meaningfully partake in any suffering, let alone those of the Awesome and Terrible Name, however we cannot as of yet cure the more devoted lemmings.

As a result of our most devoted assets in the world of academics, the philosophical outlook that has been transmitted to the majority of educated people is a horizontal outlook. They have been trained to deny the *three dimensional* reality of time as the Enemy sees it. He is outside space and time, but also present at each moment of the lived time that the humans experience. For this reason He is able to gather their offerings, however deplorable they may be, and apply them as He sees fit. His existence in an eternally present moment allows Him to be He Who was and is and is to come (if we are forced to speak this awful lyrical "beauty" as they call it). As a result, his application of graces is done in a manner that eludes our predictions. He must be cheating in some fashion — I told you, He does not play fairly.

I reread the dossier about the family that you gave me in the beginning, and I believe that our current problem is due to the mother's deceased grandmother. As much as I would like to blame you for this blunder, I myself failed to see the potential for such activity. As you know, the grandmother was from one of those Central European nations that has historically been repugnant in their fidelity to the Church. She lived through the major wars, the civil conflicts during the revolutions, and for years under the most delectable of Communist dictatorships. Through all those trials, she kept her faith like a stubborn mule. Even as we inspired the happy return of iconoclasm in churches all throughout the world, she still persisted. We leveled heresy after heresy at her from the pulpit, inspired hellishly deviant advice in the confessional, and decimated the religious orders that educated her as a girl. She watched as the Church began to implode while the ripe smoke of Satan seeped through every welcoming crack. No matter. She did what the most irritating saints always do; she embraced the Tree of Suffering.

Although we never admit this in a public fashion—don't you dare suggest to anyone I have told you this—there are some humans that we simply cannot break. Many devils have been driven to perdition as a result of contemptible souls such as this. I found the failed devil who oversaw the grandmother; he is in the Asylum and does nothing more than blabber on about his traumatic memories like a demented fool. I asked him about the woman and he shrieked like the humans do when we first introduce them to *real fire*. He was too pathetic to get any coherent information out of him. However, the warden of the Asylum presented me with the daily logs the demon recorded at the end of her life. I was correct. She offered the sufferings she endured at the end of her life from a strong cancerous disease. For reasons beyond us, this nemesis of ours chose to present her anguish to the Enemy and begged Him to apply their merits for the salvation of the children under your care. Why she chose them I do not know. But, we now have a better understanding of the force with which we are dealing.

For all the venom being funneled into the mother and father, we must act with more severity if we are to break the children. There is no option but to pull the strings with more ferocity. I haven't done this in years, but I myself will be making a visit to the family. I believe I can accelerate the process in a more lively fashion. Perhaps you may learn a thing or two from me.

Until next time,

Quelle

XVII

Malthus my boy,

I know what you are thinking, will you ever reach the level of excellence I displayed during my recent visit? It is unlikely, given that you are a fool. However, you no doubt witnessed an effective display of dynamic temptation and organization. The reason I instructed you not to take notes during my demonstration is because it was better for you to watch the event transpire without having to analyze. Knowing your demonological acumen—I still cannot believe you are the best and brightest from the Academy—you would have just confused yourself and the glorious effect of my endeavours would have been missed. Am I boasting you wonder? Yes. Yes I am. There is no place for humility in Hell. That vice the Enemy expects of his guardians and followers is nothing more than a limp excuse to revel in one's limits and failings. I am the best, the brightest and most competent devil in all the layers of our Infernal Kingdom! And you should consider yourself lucky to have witnessed such greatness in spirit.

Now, let us go through the sequence of events so that your puny mind can synthesize the importance of what happened. You will recall how I arrived; I walked right in through the front door. We are intruders to be sure, but we needn't enter into homes such as these in a clandestine fashion. When mortals commit sumptuous sins like these specimens have been doing for years, they have extended to us an invitation into their lives. Unfortunately, we still need permission to afflict the humans, but their offenses against the Enemy may as well be a welcoming-mat for our entry into their minds. We have had free reign in this home for years, especially since the father neutered himself right after the birth of the girl. The sins against the Natural Law are some of our most powerful invitations.

I did not oversee this family at that time, but in reading the reports from the previous tempters charged with their care, I was elated to read about the mother's misery from that event. She never wanted to "be done" having children, as none of the females ever really do; but she internalized the lies we have shoved down their throats like a duck being groomed for *foie gras*. She was in her early thirties when her husband castrated himself, and believed she was "doing the right thing." They had never officially agreed on a specific number of offspring, but the present culture, so galvanized by our motivations, has sold the majority of the sitting ducks in the middle class that children can only be properly raised with an enormous financial burden. This is an ahistorical fact of course, as the majority of their ancestors raised large families with little money, but it is the party line all the same. Just before the daughter was born they had committed themselves to a hefty mortgage, taking on decades of debt only surmountable by a two-income marriage. The playful irony is not lost on me that so many of these brainless twits will limit their family size in order to accrue a larger amount of wealth—in truth it is not wealth they acquire, but credit loaned from the bank—only to purchase large homes and automobiles that are empty due to their small amount of children. The power of usury never ceases crying out to Heaven and beckoning to the Gates of Hell.

Furthermore, the mother has long worshipped the actresses who somehow "get their bodies back" after producing infants. The combination of greed and vanity was too strong and she even encouraged her husband to visit the clinic for the same procedure as a house-pet. "One, two, snip!" as they say. Perhaps she did get her body back, the same body that will one day rot and putrefy with a fetid smell like a dead animal. Her story is the same as many other women, which is why our Female Vexation department inspires advertising executives to flood their television programs with commercials promoting useful messages. Have you ever noticed how during a female-oriented television programme the interruptions are filled with surgically enhanced figurines, promoting a combination of lingerie, vitality products, and diapers? In a span of three minutes we can remind the women of their internal contradictions and guilty hatred of their own decisions.

Now, back to my superior skills: what did I do when your woman was experiencing this exact situation upon my arrival? I turned her gaze towards her husband as he stood staring at his phone in the kitchen, still wearing sweat clothes from last night's sleep. Her subconscious resentment sprang into her cortex with a fever pitch. "It is really his fault I am so depressed," she thought to herself; I didn't even need to implant that thought in her mind as she has been suppressing it for years. You may recall that I immediately prompted him to raise his head and make excruciating eye-contact with her at this very moment. Both exchanged a momentary glimpse of vengeful guilt. She believed he could hear her thoughts, and his stomach dropped through the floor as he suspected she was somehow aware of his new perverted habit. Both unconsciously blaming each other for their self-disgust, both hating their very existence all the same.

You may have noticed his heart rate began to rise presently. Yes it was partly from the realization that he may eventually be caught for his new pastime, but more importantly I gave him a slight bit of prompting. I reassured him that his wife of course had no idea what he is up to, and that his wonderful little device could allow him to access his virtual harem at any moment of the day. His wife and children could be in the same room, but he can be all alone with his decomposing soul and brigade of anonymous internet prostitutes. The thrill of pornographic images for the humans is only partly about the sexual instinct; it is as much or more about the devilish desire to revel in their own filth. A man who commits to such activity becomes nothing more than a swine, rolling about in his own pathetic excrement-laden slime. Our goal is to encourage a steeper descent into the pit of self-abusive barbarism. If all goes as it should, he will come to see himself for what he truly is: *our property*.

His conscience is still not completely dead, which is why I reminded him of how thirsty he was and how satiating it would be for his throat and his vomitous guilt if he just grabbed that bottle of whiskey off the shelf. A generous gulp and he was right as rain, filled with enough liquid courage to descend into the basement bedroom he now occupies to avoid his spouse. The door was promptly locked from the inside; he has succeeded in creating his own Hell.

This man is ours, the wife is soon to be. We must now consider the next step and for how long we should keep his little hobby a secret. I think it is best to let the wounds fester, hopefully enough to cause a fatal infection. Keep the flow of shame pouring over the man, and make sure to remind him that any resistance is futile. His intellect will continue to darken to the point where he will rationalize his perversion under any circumstance. Once his intellect is in a state of full rationalization...well, then he will be as far from the Enemy as possible.

Until next time,

Quelle

XVIII

Malthus my boy,

I do hope you learned something from the master class you witnessed not only in spirit, but also had so eloquently explained to you. If there is a skill I possess that is as noteworthy as my tempting abilities, it is probably my literary acumen. I doubt there is a better author in all of Hell, no matter how many devotees of that Sartre fellow would disagree. In any case, he no longer has any time to write, what with all the daily activities we have scheduled for him. You may recall having read his hellish fiction *No Exit*, wherein he suggested that "Hell was other people." Well, in his case he was completely correct, Hell for him *is* other people. I will never tire of hearing his screams as all his damned disciples — damned as a result of internalizing his atheistic philosophy — unleash their apoplectic hysterics on him. There do not exist, I think, more enjoyable souls in Hell than those who not only ignore the Enemy, but also reject Him based on their own intellectual pretenses. The exuberant pride and egotism necessary for such a fool as the French author and others like him is so grand that it is almost deserving of a prize upon arrival. Who am I kidding! Men like him receive their reward, for we have prepared a place for them, for in our Father's house there are many pits.

Now, the delightful dunces that run the "free world" have extended this comical closure for the foreseeable future.

Amazing, every day there are a myriad of experts who adorn the television screens to give "updates" about the virus, only to restate again that their opinion is "expert," even though they admit to not understanding how the virus works. Last night as I locked myself in my chamber for covetemplation, I could not stop reveling in the irony that the majority of the human race are now hanging on every word that excretes out of the mouths of these inspired fools. Sometimes the degradation of the modern human intellect is so remarkable that I am in awe; this is easily the most gullible and debased era in the history of human intelligence. Even the pagans of antiquity, as devoted to our idols as they were, still could not be cured of their use of reason. But these humans, my boy, would believe that 2+2=5 if a celebrity or deified political figure declared it so (I heard with relish recently that the Scientism Department is on the cusp of another breakthrough in academia!). I apologize at the drips of drool that are peppered about this page, but I cannot contain myself when I contemplate the daily delivery of useful idiots who fall into our welcoming arms.

Because of this continued closure, even the majority of churches remained closed over that Mournful Day at the Empty Tomb. We may not be able to truly cancel the event, but we will always remember this great moment as a triumph. Think: the Church that was born out of resurrection from bodily death has willingly cancelled their commemoration of this terrifying event out of a fear of dying. Even more, the charlatans in control have sold the splendid lie to their disciples that they must be "obedient" as a form of piety. Of course, we cannot stand when they truthfully obey the Enemy, but it is the *world* they obey in this case. I perhaps have underestimated the effectiveness of our efforts in rewriting Church history courses in most seminaries. Apparently they have forgotten the plethora of their saints who are commemorated *because* of their courage in the face of disease and government persecution. So many of the Christian hierarchs are so uninformed that it is as if they cannot remember their own Gospel. Amazing. Some are actually claiming that the Son of the Enemy would want the idiots to stay away from their services in order to keep their bodily health. Not even our most arrogant devils would have dared propose such an unbelievable untruth, but thankfully, the humans have proposed it to themselves. There was a cleric, a Frenchman who years ago clamoured on about apostasy in the clergy, but thankfully he was largely calumniated and ridiculed. Nonetheless, it seems as though devotion to him is growing—this is a problem.

With respect to your family, the church closures have not had any real effect, although you did inform me that on Easter Sunday the mother was in a state of melancholy at the fact of having no large family gathering for the first time in her life. Normally we encourage depression and sadness, but not in this case. I am afraid that her painful nostalgia may actually work against our purposes. You see, although it is painful to admit, the Church really does animate the world, and without it there is no real meaning in their lives. It is for this reason that we prefer a mass of lukewarm Christians as opposed to outright dissenters and atheists. Those with halfhearted devotion to the Enemy will not meet His expectations, but since they are generally convinced that they *are* pleasing to Heaven, they are less likely to see themselves for the sinners we love them to be. The lukewarm believers are easily accessible to us because they live in a state of contradiction; outwardly they convince themselves they are on the Enemy's team, but inwardly they are easily manipulated in our direction.

In any case, the calendar year is, despite the efforts of our beloved French Republic, completely dependent on the Church and her festivals. It does put us at a disadvantage in many cases. Even for the most wretched of sinners, we cannot hide the blasted warmth of Christmas Eve, or the punishing hope of Easter. In the best case we can foment a greater anger in the souls of apostate believers. We do this by convincing them that the Church has fooled them into a painful need for a celebration that is ultimately based on a myth. As a result they experience a sort of despair that their childlike longing for family and celebration is nothing but a superstitious illusion.

I believe the woman is experiencing the general melancholy and not the rage we prefer. She is of the emotional sort and believes her feelings can say true things to her about reality. Feelings are highly useful in a human predisposed to our devices, but since the vermin are in fact physical creatures, their emotions can elicit in even the worst of them little pricks of conscience and longing for eternal things. She now sees her place in relation to the Church as if she were on the outer rings of fading concentric circles in a pool of still water; she knows not why she aches for the focal point in the centre, but she cannot help thinking that if she edges any further, she will perish.

She is in a dangerous place, and how you respond to this may determine her fate, but more importantly, it may determine yours. You must ensure that while she is in this state, which may last for a day or two, that she not be presented with any concrete material that brings her mind to contemplate the Enemy in her soul. She is still so enwrapped in the effects of her participation in the New Age that she is fortunately impervious to any logical arguments in favour of Christianity that use reason; however her emotional state is at a pinnacle right now and she could be swayed by anything sentimental. It is a constant back and forth with these humans, just when we think we have them fooled by argumentation, they can be swayed by innate yearnings that the Enemy unfortunately planted on their hearts. That dreaded Augustine used to go on about the heart being restless until it finds its rest *in* the Enemy (the human obsession with beauty is intolerable). It is nothing more than selfishness.

I am going to suggest something that may confuse you, but believe me it is exactly what we need right now. She is so repulsed by logical thinking, as it does nothing for her flighty sensibilities, therefore your task is to *not* distract her if her son—who is more and more theologically dangerous every day—approaches her to speak about religion. He is thinking too clearly for her, thus his arguments and adolescent zeal will come off as dispassionate and unattractive. If he does approach her during this period, remind her that *she* is in charge, and he is but a pubescent weasel, and she must not listen to his immature babble. We are in a tricky position, but we will see this through. Never let your guard down, remember; the Guardians know just as much as we, and although the mother ignores hers, the son is fully aware of the reality of his.

Until next time,

Quelle

XIX

Malthus my boy,

I cannot blame you for this specific issue that we now face, although your periodic bungling up until this point has made this more likely. I debated as to whether this was the moment where I should finally end your career, however the situation is too delicate and we are in too far. Replacing you with someone else would do me no good at this time, and as much fun as I had the other day on the ground, I will not be blamed for this if things are not remedied. This is your bed; you have made it and now you will sleep in it, for better or for worse. The pressure is on my boy. If you right the ship, I will look like a master for mentoring you; if you fail I will ensure that The Powers that Be know exactly how much you are at fault.

The mother said a prayer with her son and daughter. Not any prayer, but that excruciating angelic salutation and petition and praise to the Fearful Incarnation. She said only one, but one is sometimes all that is needed to scuttle our plans. To be fair you did follow my orders from the last letter and kept her mind off of harmful contemplations of the Enemy, even during her most melancholic moments. And you did prepare her for an ignition of prideful resistance to any logical argument in favour of the Christian position. However, she was led by a certain instinct that we can rarely root out of a person.

The reason you could not think or act clearly as she approached her son's room is easily explained. That blasted melody and poetic cadence that evoked a sickening gentleness is called Chant. The boy and his sister were watching a presentation of the Sacrifice on his computer, and the deafening harmony that emanated into the hallway was the music that accompanied the liturgy. I understand you have heard of this during your education, but it is so excruciating, even paralysing, that you never learn it by experience until you are in the field. Furthermore, we cannot bring ourselves to recreate it, as it is too painful and dreadful. It has a double effect; on the one hand it provides a repulsive protection against our advances, and on the other hand it hypnotizes humans for the Enemy's purposes. It does not attract all humans I might add, for those who are deeply reprogrammed by our exquisite atonal noise, the simplicity of Chant actually hurts their heads. Alas, the mother is not one of these helpful heathens. Her internal homesickness primed her for an effortless reception, which is why even a faint flickering of that abhorrent sound was enough to redirect her on her way to her bedroom.

We have achieved great levels of success during the closures of churches sponsored by Church and State, but the transmission of services by way of electronic communication has unfortunately spread a visual representation of the most ancient liturgies. Our liturgical expert, the Son of Baal, did extraordinary work to dismantle the primary rituals of the Church some decades ago. The results have been outstanding. However, as the believers become whittled down to a more dedicated and resilient bunch, their curiosity for all but forgotten traditions has grown miserably. The altered rituals suffice during in-person services, but their aesthetic deficiencies are too obviously grotesque when placed on film. As a result, many with no previous desire for antiquated memorials have gravitated to the rites they believe are more aesthetically pleasurable. Many of the Christians have never attended an event such as these, thankfully. But, the mother was reminded of her grandmother's funeral—which was done according to the older lamentable rubrics—when she heard that particular tone wafting out of the room.

There was, I admit, little you could do when this happened. If only the boy had turned off the video when his mother waltzed into the room, but instead he just stared at her while she gazed at the screen as if watching a resurrected ancestor.

We still cannot build anything that legitimately competes with what the humans consider true beauty. At best we can exalt distracting elements and focal points in order to have a person contemplate fleeting things. The modern liturgy still contains that detestable Sacrifice, but it is happily hidden in a noisy affair that focuses on man, with everything on a horizontal plane. The congregants may parrot a variety of pious responses to the priest in the contemporary rubrics, but when he says "lift up your hearts," they mutter their futile jargon while staring a man straight in the face. The rites from antiquity were inspired by the Son Himself, and therefore all attention is taken off of the mundane and the believers are forced to look higher during periods of quiet reverence. Do you see how dangerous this is? Although the mother was not there in person, the experience stood in such stark contrast to the useful ugliness of her life.

It is a double-edged sword you see; on the one hand we have made the world and liturgy uglier than it has ever been, but on the other hand this means that relics of an ancient aesthetic and purity capture the attention of unprepared humans with unfortunate effectiveness. As I mentioned earlier, the mother has not been sufficiently reprogrammed in order that she may properly detest this sort of beauty. Ironically if she were a frequent church-goer at a location that utilizes ceremonial novelties, we would have had a better shot at repulsing her in this instance. I cannot tell you how exquisite it is to witness those who profess devotion to the Enemy become agitated when they attend the same liturgy that all of their saints and grandparents frequented. Some of the most fruitful episodes of uncharity have taken place on behalf of those who have grown accustomed to the new routines. It is as if they truly believe that their Church began but a few decades ago, and that anything opposed to the current manifestation—a manifestation that has splendidly increased the auto-destruction of the Church—is somehow against the Enemy's wishes. The internal inconsistency necessary to unyieldingly defend a representation of their religion that is also the cause or symptom of the religion's steep decline, is extraordinary. There are even believers and clerics who actively advocate *against* the ancient languages in their rites. They express an idea that has no basis in real facts, that apparently the pagans of the world will respond better if the faith is presented in their tongue. I adore these useful idiots, they ignore history, tradition, and even basic statistical analysis; they do our job for us.

For all the good we have done in confusing the Christians about their own worship, this generation of neo-pagans we have produced is lamentably susceptible to the old tactics that plagued our efforts during the horrible periods of mass conversion. I am afraid there may be more like the mother if this sort of thing continues, and we must act quickly within this household if we are to kibosh any further advance. Doubtless the son is over the moon that his mother has softened to his position, even to the point of saying a prayer with him and his sister. If we had control over him at this time I would encourage him to level a barrage of apologetics in her direction as a way of overwhelming her delicate state.

I will consult my old mentor straight away and come up with a plan. For the moment continue with the normal temptations in an unrelenting fashion in hopes that a fatigue of resistance will have an effect. Also, keep an extremely close eye on the son, he is no doubt scheming as to how he can trap his mother in the Enemy's camp. Send me word immediately if anything troubling arises.

Until next time,

Quelle

XX

You wretched imp.

If what you tell me is true, then we may lose the mother. I cannot stand this young man, this adolescent nemesis who acts nothing like his peers! Why can he not just acquiesce to our advances? What is it about his sickening devotion that allows him to avoid the blitz of artillery that swallows up the vast majority of his generation? He should be prideful, he should be effeminate, he should not contain such quiet wisdom and poise in his dealings with his own mother. He deals with her in a putrid and priestly manner. Never in my career have I witnessed such an inexplicable delicacy of approach by such a zealous and inexperienced youth. He does not argue with her on religion, he does not push his advances against her; he simply prays for her and *loves* her (revolting). Oh Hell! I cannot abide this abomination any longer. Now you tell me that in the short time since we last spoke, the mother has agreed to visit the priest and make her first general confession. If this tragedy comes to pass and we lose her to the Enemy, make no mistake I will blame everything on you.

We have done everything in our power to utilize the stupidity of the statesmen and Church hierarchs during this inverted quarantine, so that the Sacraments are practically unavailable. Priests all over the world have been forbidden by civil and ecclesial command to attend to their flock, yet by some sort of intolerable coincidence, the boy has found priests who *obey the Enemy more than man.* These unbearable clergymen care nothing for worldly acceptance or even their reputation amongst other churchmen. We have organized perhaps the most ingenious persecution of the Christians to date, one wherein the thought of them uniting in any form of worship is not only seen as nonessential, but even dangerous to public health. In the past we have fomented useful hatred of what they believe, but never anything so useful as labeling them as agents of viral dissemination by the plain act of congregating.

I knew that boy's teacher would come back to haunt us; in that short time he spent brainwashing the son he sparked an insatiable rage against Hell and sin in his heart. His simple suggestion to the boy that he consult those blasted "traditional" priests has been as responsible for this butterfly effect as anything. There remains only a short while until the scheduled Sacrament, and we must act in a way that stops this once and for all. Fortunately, we still have the father tightly in our grasp. I am going to explain to you exactly what you must do. This may be our last option.

The mother and father are still in a state of resentment and silence, and the children—although they pray for their father—are not unaware of the dire situation the marriage is in. They may be on the Enemy's side for now, but the influence a father has over his home is invaluable. Even with a pious mother and pious children, a fiendish father can thrust his offspring into our net at any moment. Like the plethora of priests who have damned practically whole congregations, the father of a home can do the same to his household. The man is in a state of such a spiritual and moral decay that we must unleash the totality of his Satanic stench on the others.

His addiction to evil images is so fruitful that the perverted visages are all he thinks about. Combined with his functional alcoholism, he is rarely coherent around his family and locks himself in his room for hours. The children are confused but in their blasted innocence do not expect their father to have such a victorious vice as he does. The wife however (although she may not know for certain), certainly has her suspicions. She may seem as if she is under a certain spell in Heaven's favour, but at the moment she is still not in a state of reconciliation. The particular graces she accesses at the moment do not give the Enemy entrance to dwell in her soul. If we can force her husband's hand and wrench him into a position that takes control of the atmosphere of the entire home, then we still stand a chance.

Now, the time has come for the husband's habit to be made manifest for all to see. Normally I would recommend a long-term festering of his self-abusive devotion, which in reality would give us great pleasure for years to come. I actually prefer that the male humans develop manageable vices such as his, in order that they live a long life full of little slips and lies without ever experiencing excessive prompting from their conscience. If we were not in this position I might even tell you to have the man take a step back from his habit, but we are in need of a *nuclear option*.

We still have the reality of the failing marriage on our side. For this reason we must facilitate an irreparable schism between the mother and father. I believe that we have the ammunition to do so. It is a bit of a risk however, because whenever we force explosive conflict between spouses there is always the possibility of empathy and reconciliation. But his drinking habit and pleasant perversion has rendered him completely callous and self-involved. He is diving deeper into more violent genres, and his continued unemployment and financial anxiety has further developed. In all my years I have never seen a man in his sort of situation who could respond any differently than I expect him to. He will undoubtedly blame the woman for his faults, and insult her in a manner so exquisite that he may as well be repeating the wrathful musings of our favourite damned residents. His current disposition is one wherein, during moments of conflict, he will lay all blame for his own faults on his wife, which is why we must now act in an opportune fashion.

How do we pull off such a maneuver? It is not that hard. You must remember, the man is nothing more than a walking corpse at this point. His intellect has been deadened due to his increasing sinfulness, and he has become numb. He will not fight for his marriage, because he will not fight for anything. A man who has given into his most animal appetites goes from being a man to a wonderfully effeminate limpnoid, and now we get to enjoy him like a cat with a dead rodent.

I mentioned some letters ago that the usage of sexualized images has narcotic effects on the user similar to other drugs that tickle the degenerate fancies of the participant; this means that with every up there is a down, and after the elation comes a state of self-loathing. With this particular activity, there is an added moral dimension that ruminates in the deadened conscience, as every man knows he is committing adultery of some sort when he indulges. As a result, each man knows he is a criminal and deserves a punishment. However, those far from the Enemy do not seek to repent—thanks be to our Father Below—but instead they seek to *justify*. Justification of one's own failings can come in a variety of forms, but for our purposes it is relevant to focus on the act of projecting one's guilt onto another.

As the man wallows in his fallen and shameful filth after partaking, you may effortlessly draw his attention to all the things he resents about his wife: she has not "met his needs," she is a prude, she is selfish, she is illogical, she looks down on him, and so on. It is not even necessary for his ideas of her to be true, all that matters is that he can convince himself that she is to blame. The woman has a co-worker, a man, of whom she has spoken fondly before, perhaps this man could be imagined as a threat. For all your man knows, maybe his wife has been having an affair with him for years, it does not matter that it is fiction. All that matters is that his rage and emotions are whipped into a volatile cocktail with enough strength to inflict fatal marital damage. This rage gives him pleasure, but it also causes him harm, which means he will simultaneously indulge the feeling, but also want the feeling to end. A most pitiful man and a tasty specimen.

Due to this imagined affair—that did not exist until five minutes prior—he will be in a fighting mood and therefore can be agitated into a seemingly petty altercation with his wife. They are still rarely speaking, so when they do fight, his volatility will catch her off guard in a way that frightens her. She will react with severity as a form of self-defence, and within a short time they will be hurling insults back and forth. What a perfect moment this will be to remind her of the time he spends locked in the basement, or the obsession he now has with guarding his mobile phone. "What is he hiding? For what reason does he cling to that device like a dog to a bone?" She may be an idiot, but even she possesses enough brain matter to solve this obvious riddle; he is enslaved to the solitary vice.

Her stomach will sink through the floor and she will feel as if she is standing in the room with an intruder. "This is not the man I married," she will say to herself, but you will reply,

"This is *exactly* the man you married." She will inevitably ask him in a quiet voice to explain what he has been up to, but he will not answer. Immediately she will shriek like a melodramatic windbag, demanding that he tell her the truth. It does not matter if he replies or not, his silence will suffice for consent. Hysterical women are masochists, and they obsessively dig deeper and deeper into their own gaping wounds. "How many times!" she will probe, "what sort of stuff are you watching? Let me see your phone! I want to see!" Depending on her disposition she will either shrink into a deeper depression, or lash out with whatever weapon she has. Hopefully she will belittle him in ways that shorten him to the size of the rat he is.

Now, at this moment you must pay attention to his interior dialogue, because something quite peculiar will take place; he will actually experience a moment of relief. This moment will be short lived as he watches the nuptial murder of the woman he promised to "have and to hold." He will finally see that he is not even a man; he is a monster. If you arrange the event to happen in front of the children, I may even have to suggest a promotion for you.

Oh we do get to have a bit of fun in our line of work don't we?

Act now.

Quelle

XXI

Malthus my boy,

I had my doubts about you, Malthus, and throughout this process I did not think you would secure the family as you have. But, you have surprised us all and now stand in a victorious position as master and commander of this family. Since your recent triumph I have been celebrating heavily, and we will one day celebrate even harder when the members of this family descend deep into our pit. You somehow managed to dislodge your head from your posterior cavern and follow my instructions to the letter. I must admit, watching you carry out our last plan was some of the most effective and dynamic destruction I have ever had the pleasure to see. You orchestrated every single aspect exactly as I would have, and you even found a way to add your own personal flare. I suggested you have the children present for the display, but you went a step further and even had the mother bring the children into the mayhem. She presented good old dad as a villain — superb.

The look on the young girl's face when it was in fact *she* who was prompted to prod her father about his perverted video habit…Well, I will never forget that pain and anguish, it is a highlight of my career. Think: the girl used to look up at her father, but now she cannot even look *at him*. He reacted just as I suspected and proved himself to be a sullen weasel, incapable of boasting of his crimes with any gusto. He had not even the courage to lie out of self preservation. With the mother sobbing and the girl breathless with disbelief, you engineered a perfectly timed offensive of self-hatred and instant thoughts of suicide in the father. Magnificent! All the while the son stood there, unsure of what to do, feeling as if he should do something yet incapable of saying a word. You assessed his interior disposition perfectly and saw that minuscule crack in his resolve, giving you just enough room to sew a perfectly placed seed of doubt. "How is this happening to our family if I have prayed so hard?" he thought. Brilliance! Clearly I have taught you well. The mother shrieked and went on and on about divorce. The husband emasculated himself even further by breaking down into tears, squealing like a pig being slaughtered. He was so pitiful in that moment that I had to look away, it was too nauseating to even pay attention to the blabber that came out of his mouth.

Parents are the whole world to their children and when we facilitate the destruction of the parental unit, well, we may as well be splitting apart the foundations of the earth on which they stand. The Enemy created this ghastly unit as a way to raise and protect more offspring. Once we get rid of the parents, then the way is open to devour the tender little ones like so much juicy meat. At the moment when their marriage shattered, a thousand demons were instantly racing toward the children. That titillating sight never gets old.

And what happened next was the most delightful thing of all, touching on our old nemesis. Late into the evening of the marital schism, the boy angrily went to confront his father in his basement abode. The young man may have been frustratingly pious, but he is still a teenager, and therefore always susceptible to volatile outbursts. He had it in his mind that he would "tear a strip" off the old-man, but instead he found him in a dead-sleep, no doubt from the healthy portion of liquor he was accustomed to drinking in the evening. As you know, rage is a vehicle for a sort of unholy pleasure if we guide it correctly. There is such a thing as righteous anger, very rare amongst the humans nowadays, but the boy did not have nearly the level of self-control needed to keep his anger holy. He was in a destructive mood, and he needed to break something. As he saw the man lying there, a drunken adulterer, he imagined harming his father for just a brief moment in time. He was horrified with himself, but he also felt a touch of exhilaration at the power he had in that moment over the man he now blamed for the escalating downfall of his family life. The first instance of patricidal hatred was involuntary, and therefore not a sin, but the second instance was exquisitely volitional and he *enjoyed* the feeling. As he stood there staring at the sad excuse for a man that is his father, his heart raced and his breathing grew frantic as he imagined ways he would beat the man into a pulp. You understood well the implications of this moment, and saw a chasm in his defences due to the commission of his first grave sin in some time. Beside the lifeless body of the fallen patriarch, sat his open computer. The son was so consumed with his rage when he entered the room, that the white-noise of his hatred hid the bestial sounds bellowing forth from the device. As he caught his breath he noticed the sound and turned his attention to the screen and saw it all. With surgical precision you pounced on this opportunity to redirect his hatred of his father inward; the poisonous seed of self-abuse was planted deep into his mind. He then committed another mortal sin — he did not look away. I rejoiced when I found out he had fallen! Keep pouring the shame and self-hatred down upon him like so much acid rain to melt his sentimental piety. All you need to do now is convince him that he can't resist and that he is too evil for confession. They practically damn themselves if they believe that. Then the evil images can be embedded deep within his psyche and eventually destroy his intellect that once had faith, causing him a complete loss of all light of reason. We've done it so many times to the great damned souls from sins of the flesh which is an ideal conduit to Atheism. It's like clockwork.

To our continued pleasure, the mother has proven serious about the divorce and is fomenting insurrection against the father with each passing moment. Whatever longing she may have had for heavenly things is gone. She is now a snake full of venom, a fire-breathing dragon hell-bent on destroying every aspect of the man. I must say she evokes a certain excitement in me. As the Church approaches that awful feast commemorating the *tongues of fire*, her mouth continues to spew flaming darts of belittling insults and castrating calumnies. You need not guide her in the slightest, she is a culmination of feminist rage and self-righteous egotism. She has even begun bashing the man to her friends and has started sharing ridiculous messages on her internet groups, droning about independence and girl power. Women are so predictable these days, years of usurpation and self-aggrandizement has led them to justify all their pitiable decisions by vomiting slogans about "empowerment" and "self-discovery." Mark my words, now that the strict measures of their state shutdowns are lifting, she will spend night after night drinking wine with her closest companions, while they justify her every decision and the dissolution of her marriage. "You finally have a chance to make your own way," they will say, and "you are a strong and independent woman, you won't be held back now."

I do love the nonsense the females tell each other to condone all manner of imbecility. They have swallowed the lies we have transmitted for decades through the mouths of our most precious she-devils and popular psychologists on television broadcasts. They actually believe that divorce is sometimes "healthy" for their children, and that they can remain friends with their former spouse. She definitely will make her own way now — she will make her way into a life of increasing loneliness and despair, and we will make our way deeper into her. Furthermore, her apparent independence is one of our greatest assets; she is now independent from any stability and therefore will become easily dependent on whatever supposed panacea promises to fix her problems. The New Age philosophies with which she has heretofore only dabbled will offer her a plethora of self-help books that effectively trick the minds of hoards of females, with pseudo-religious psychological lunacy. She has no real money to speak of, and therefore encouraging her to ruthlessly annihilate her husband throughout arbitration will be a breeze. Even better, she may convince herself that a way to find temporal happiness will be to "have a fling" with a man she finds attractive. In reality any sexual dalliance with a strange man will only plunge her into a deeper and more fruitful depression.

Given that the husband is unemployed without any real prospects, he will be forced to move in with his parents. Multigenerational living used to be normal for the humans, and it was in fact a problem for our purposes as the family unit was thereby strengthened. However, a grown son living with his elderly parents in today's world is seen by many as a humiliating shame. No doubt the mother will do everything she can to scuttle any attempt of the children spending significant time with him, and he will therefore be utterly alone and isolated. Lick your lips Malthus, he will be your dinner guest.

The way things stand, it will be hard for the children to blame anyone other than their father for the dissolution of the family. His are the most visible transgressions, and the children are not privy to the private resentments both parents harboured for some time. It is useful to escalate their blind allegiance to the mother, because although it will deepen a bond between her and the children, eventually they will see she is as much to blame as anyone. Give it a few years, in time they will see how pitiful she is. So often in these divorced families there is an undulation between parental allegiance as conflicts illuminate varying personality flaws at opportune times.

Due to the virus it seems the schools and all youth activities are effectively closed until autumn. This is excellent. Their current schooling is a bore, and there is very little they can do to socialize outside of the home. There will be no escape and no support for them for the foreseeable future. Even their grandparents are off limits as the mother barred the children—who are not ill in the slightest—from visiting the elderly. I say, more souls have died alone as a result of the hysterical reaction to this never-ending flu season than perhaps any other time in human history. I recently read a report that contained promising statistics demonstrating the exponential rise in Christians dying with the priests locked out of the hospitals and nursing homes. And to think, even many of their bishops are compliant. To say this era has been a triumph is an understatement.

A year from now the previous lifestyle of the family will be but a painful memory; a painful memory that you should continually exploit. The father will undoubtedly be living in some cheap apartment building, struggling to find a job that pays as his last one did. The mother will have to downsize to a smaller home as well, and relocate to a place she does not like. She will of course convince the children she is happy, but it will be a lie. The children will either abandon their faith entirely, or keep some lukewarm milquetoast version that will inevitably decay through an adolescence full of mortal sin. We have word that the school teacher who so greatly influenced the boy is no longer with the institution, so there is no longer a worry of any education that would please the Enemy. Even better, children who watch their parents sever the family into pieces are rarely emotionally stable. This means that it is a matter of time before they latch on to some ill-advised behaviour that builds a habit of vice. The lack of a father in the home almost always results in girls becoming victims of poor relationships. As for boys, they often build up anger that turns them into delinquents of some sort. Their school performance will suffer, and their pleasure seeking behaviour will increase. Do what I say and each miscreant will go into the divorce as one sort of child, and come out as *our sort of child*.

I could go on, but you get the point. You have won Malthus, well, I have won through you, and without me you would be shrieking in agony for our amusement. There is no need for me to continue corresponding with you as often as we have, you can now have your fun and finish the job in your own time and manner. You now have at your disposal a number of humans to torment and guide on a slow and gradual descent into the fire. Even a devil capable of the blunders you have demonstrated would have a hard time failing to harvest this crop. I have heard rumblings that I will be assigned a new apprentice very shortly, and therefore will need to devote my time elsewhere. I will inform the relevant authorities that you are now on your own. As is customary, I will check in with you in a few months, but you must inform me if anything changes between now and then that requires a higher level of expertise. That being said, do not bother me with trivial matters that I have already explained.

Enjoy yourself Malthus.

Until next time,

Quelle

Attn: Blockleiter
Tribunal for the Discipline of Delinquent Devils
6662 Undying Worm
The Pit

At the request of the Administration in the ongoing case of the devil called Malthus, I will present in the following report all the information needed to lock that disappointing failure away forever. Before I continue, I must admit that the information herein will cause the Tribunal great displeasure. From my research and from the testimony of my agents in the field, I have compiled a comprehensive report of the most horrifying details pertaining to the state of the family formerly under Malthus' care. I believe that, although this report is painful to read, the information will help inspire a proper application of the measures necessary. If it is painful for the members of this Tribunal to hear this letter, believe me, it is ever more painful for me to relay the relevant points.

I trust you have read the correspondence between myself and Malthus during the major portion of our working relationship. As you have seen, the situation undulated between victory and defeat. If it were not for my expert guidance it is certain that Malthus would have lost the family straight away. If there is anything commendable in him as a tempter it is what he learned from me. (As an aside, we must deal with the Academy and the consistent lowering of the calibre of operatives that graduate from that institution. The happy lowering of the moral standard of the human race has come at a certain cost it seems; there is less urgency to improve the devils as they face little to no resistance in the field.)

At any rate, because of my efforts and Malthus' eventual acquiescence to my authority, the family was nicely tucked away under our cloven hooves. The father became the most

118

delectable of perverts, the mother turned the children against the father, and the children fell into interior torment and moral decay. Within mere weeks of the pinnacle moment that saw the family so playfully severed in two, the family was a complete wreck. The father was unceremoniously scuttled out of the house like a tenant without rent money, only to find himself sleeping in his elderly parents' basement. In our eyes he continued to improve in his consumption of both drink and pornographic material. He was isolated from his children, and his children hated him.

The mother of course did exactly as I said she would, and through a series of self-help books, New Age superstitions and feminist mantras she settled nicely into an interior decline. Of course she lied to all who knew her by sharing images of herself socializing with other "singles," along with quotes from our most useful celebrities prattling on about empowerment and self-worth. As with all parental separations, the children were largely forgotten. They did what most children from these situations do, and concealed their depression in order to try and convince their parents that they were not actually suffering. These sorts of parents are always riddled with overwhelming guilt, and therefore welcome the fictitious dispositions of their offspring as a way of appeasing their consciences.

Being a book-worm, the daughter retreated into literature. Fortunately, she meandered into the world of the young-adult books which we have promoted for years, and was therefore being well-groomed for sexual exploitation and emotional wounds. She lost herself in the world of modern fantasy novels and eventually the film versions of those novels. There is a great danger when the humans read the old fantasy tales that come from the minds of Christian authors; the mind of a child

119

really is our great battle ground, and there is almost nothing worse than a child who makes sense of the world with the images of Christian folklore. However, the contemporary stories of fantasy come from a neo-pagan world that has lost any real sense of the Christian moral order. All their fallen and degenerate fantasies come to life in the form of vampires and wizards, with pages full of consequentialist morality and sexualized undertones. The darkness that fills these pages inculcates in the young reader a certain hopelessness and preternatural negativity. The girl became utterly addicted to these stories and they became her scriptures. In addition, she was embarrassed by her mother's behaviour and sought to avoid any conversation of substance with her. Her faith was largely guided by her brother, and his delectable fall pushed her over the edge.

The son continued to descend into our grasp, and as a result of his mounting self-abuse, he quickly disposed of that awful habit of praying the beads. As his hatred for his father grew, he bathed more and more in that glorious vomit of pornography that captured his father for us. He allowed in our operatives who redirected his adolescent zeal for the Enemy into a splendid passion for individualist philosophy. He did not become an atheist in the full sense of the word, nevertheless he found a useful consolation in that growing neo-paganism and humanism that dominates the philosophical landscape for men of this age. He developed an obsession with Vikings and evolution, and began researching the use of psychedelic potions and chemicals as a way of "expanding his consciousness." This family was ours, all ours, and Malthus had perhaps the easiest path to a lasting victory that I have seen in all my years.

Nonetheless, the good news stops there and the torment begins here. You will recall from my last letter written to Malthus that during the explosive break up of the family, the father broke down and squealed like a stuck pig. It was too much to bear and I could not pay attention for a brief moment in time. Now, I was present to observe the fun and was not an active participant, as this was ultimately Malthus' operation and not mine. Following the necessary protocols, Malthus had one of his subordinates taking notes about the interior dialogue of the afflicted humans. Well, apparently during that moment, the father was so ashamed with himself that he was for a moment actually humble. In the notes recently acquired from the note-taking tempter we read the following: *in the quiet of his mind, during a time of extreme anguish, the man uttered an ambiguous prayer, the contents of which was "Help me L*#d."* This note was included in the report of the incident with a commentary that disregarded it as a desperate act and not an honest request to the Enemy.

However, it turns out it *was* a real prayer, although seemingly insignificant. I told that blasted idiot to keep watch for the tricks of the Guardians, but he failed to plan adequately for their unfair dealings. In that minuscule moment of pitiful pandering to the Enemy, the Guardian of the father, ever ready to pounce on any inkling of permission, immediately used this as an opportunity to redirect this petition. In that annoying manner of moving on the edge of space and time, the father's thought was immediately shared from his Guardian to the Guardian of the boy's teacher whom they had not seen for months. If you are wondering how I have received such accurate information from the Enemy camp, well, they have permitted us to see it in order to torture us.

Now, the teacher was seemingly out of the picture, but apparently he has this habit of praying for his students and their families, especially if he suspects they are troubled. Since he left the school, he heard of the troubles facing the family during the shut-down and directed most of his efforts to their intercession. As a result, he was afflicted with the deepest sorrow when his Guardian made manifest to him that the boy's family was suffering some great calamity. Being a traditional believer, he began a series of petitionary prayers and mortifications for the spiritual head of the family, the father... We all know how dangerous this is. He offered his Sacramental reception for him, and begged the Enemy to give the man a sign that would rip him from our grasp.

Malthus, the complete and utter imbecile, was so infatuated with his merrymaking that he did nothing but push more and more pornographic material on the father. Of course, the father did continue for a time in this arena of sin, but Malthus was overbearing and short sighted in his approach. With each passing week, and every new prayer by the teacher, the father became more and more disgusted with himself. It is often a good thing when the afflicted humans despise themselves, but it can be dangerous if someone is praying for them. Since the man was under a relentless assault of highly dangerous petitionary prayers, he began to see things differently. Previously, during his more vulnerable moments after drinking and self-medication, he would distract himself from his conscience by further debauchery or with some meaningless entertainment. But, since the state of vulnerability is fertile soil for the Enemy, the man started to switch his emotional disposition from a place of shame and self-loathing to a place of guilt and sorrow. In a way, his pleasures ceased to be pleasures, and he even started to grow tired of them.

Keep in mind that the man was out of work and now faced the prospect of a financially crippling divorce. Well, as the government welfare assistance ran out, the man was desperate for a job. There was no work available in his field of expertise, which Malthus should have used as a way to increase resentment in his soul. Yet again, the imp was lazily launching hedonist temptations his way, all the while the man was growing more and more tired of these things. The teacher never ceased to pray for him, and began praying daily a terrifying chaplet to that Angel whom we dare not name. Everyday the General stormed our efforts with a relentless cavalry of soldiers in the Heavenly Host who used every trick in the book. They played harps and sang hymns, they sounded trumpets and prayed without ceasing; in the most disorienting moments they even launched fiery arrows of conquering humility and a spirit of repentance into the man's soul. It was as ghastly an offensive as you can imagine.

The Guardians began to coordinate the workings of their obedient humans, therefore various believers kept crossing paths with the father. Eventually he encountered one such man who opened the flood gates of irreparable damage. Out of desperation for employment, he reluctantly interviewed for an agricultural labour position, even though he has historically been the furthest thing from the type of man who works hard for a living. The farmer who offered the employment is one of those remnant Christians who still fill the rural areas of most human societies. Unmoved by our secularist philosophies and unsympathetic to the religious aversion of most modern people, he displays an overbearing statue of the Woman in his office. Rather than being repulsed by such a thing upon entering the office for the interview, the man formerly under Malthus' care was mesmerized. The man noticed a sense of tranquility in his soul that he had not felt since he was a child. At one point the farmer even had to repeat an interview question multiple times, due to the man's hypnotized gaze directed towards the statue. Even worse, the farmer did not see this as a problem. He looked over his shoulder to see what the man was so infatuated with, and immediately understood what had happened. He hired the man on the spot, even without finishing the interview, declaring in the most nauseating fashion, "The L*#d has sent you here for a reason, can you start now?" I hate this sort of human! They do not think for themselves, instead they hang off of every prompting that emanates forth from the Celestial Kingdom.

The man was overwhelmingly confused and did not know how to process such a strange event. That same morning he awoke with his head aching, and his mouth dry and fuzzy from a considerable amount of whiskey. In addition, he felt that continual lump of guilt in his throat from his ever increasing conscience. All of a sudden, he now found himself staring at an image of that Immaculate Woman, and for the first time in months he was not tormented by an endless mental loop of nameless sirens from our videos. The disorienting quiet of mind he was feeling only made him more open to accept a job he did not even want in the first place.

That day he performed back-breaking labour until well after the sun had set. His hands were pulverized by blisters, his feet burned in his boots, and he had never worked up an appetite so fierce in his life. What's worse, he was so distracted by the all encompassing tasks at hand, that he could not find time to think. He simply worked, and as a result he was... happy. For the first time in years he was simply happy. He did not think of pleasure or money, or drinking, or even his failed marriage. As he arrived home that night, it was all he could do to hoover down any food he could find, and his fatigue was so great that he just went to bed. He did not watch any videos, he did not even have a drink! His physical exhaustion was so strong that he forgot about himself. Even more troubling, he slept through the night, deeply and awoke feeling rested. He was even excited to get back to work the next day, and took a certain satisfaction in his aches and blisters. "There is something meaningful about this pain," he said to himself. Disgusting.

Though he was inexperienced, the farmer believed he was doing the Enemy's wishes by hiring him, and therefore he was patient with the man, treating him as an apprentice. Since the farmer did not have to answer to any of the politically correct overlords we inspire, he said whatever he wanted to while they worked. He talked about the Church, morality, prayer and family. He even said prayers before eating when they stopped for meals. His children often came out to see him during the day, and his daughters would accompany them in the tractors while they harvested well into the night. The frequent presence of children, combined with the fact that the atmosphere was dastardly Christian, meant that the man only spoke of things he knew were moral—things he began to believe himself. He admired the farmer, and looked up to him as some sort of model for manhood. Oh how I prefer effeminate men.

I told you the story would be painful, but it gets worse. Remember that all the rage you are embracing is to be directed at Malthus, as this is his fault. I informed Malthus to tell me if any drastic changes had taken place, but he did not. Why he thought I would not find out is beyond me, but again, this generation of devils is increasingly stupid.

As I mentioned, the various Guardians and Angels were working together under the guidance of the General. These villains orchestrated things in such a way that totally evaded the dimwitted oversight of the devil under investigation. After some time, the man developed a friendship with the agriculturist and was invited to spend an evening with him and his family at the end of one of their busy periods. Upon entering the home, the man was stopped in his tracks by an atmosphere that would repel even the most seasoned of tempters. Before he could get his boots off he was confronted with two little twin girls, no more than four years of age, with matching hairstyles and pink dresses. Their eyes opened wider than should be humanly possible, they greeted him with smiles and called him "Sir." Feeling dizzy from the devastating waft of pure childlike innocence, he put his hand on the wall while he untied his lace. As he stood up a young man of twelve years old approached with his younger brother in tow. The preteen shook his hand and looked him in the eye; he had the impression that he was staring at a man wiser than himself, although 30 years his junior.

The home itself is over a century old and each doorway is adorned with heirloom trinkets of the Conqueror hanging from the Excruciating Weapon, with statues and paintings of our most hated adversaries spread throughout. The smell of what came from the stove brought back a damnable nostalgia that immediately transported the man as if bilocating, to a moment in his childhood. This caused a great ache and longing in his heart for an innocence he had forgotten was possible. Upon entering the kitchen he, for a moment, lost his breath as he laid eyes upon the mother of the home. She was setting the table with an infant asleep against her body, wrapped tightly against her beating heart. This wretched woman is a model of Christian chastity and the elevated presence of her virtue struck the man to his core. He looked at the twin girls as they ran about the kitchen singing a nursery rhyme, and realized in an instant that they and their mother were one and the same. They were pure and undefiled, like animated copies of that statue he saw in the office. Every single infernal temptress he gawked at for the last few months flooded to his mind. This time, however, it caused him pain and not pleasure. He could have vomited if he allowed himself. He thought of his daughter and his wife, he thought of his mother. He immediately hated lust, he hated pornography, he hated his actions. The worst thing possible had happened; he was convicted of the full reality of sin. Without an audible cry, he did not merely beg the Enemy for help like he did when all our work began to crumble, no, he begged for *forgiveness*.

In reality this moment lasted but a matter of seconds, but he regained awareness of his presence in the room after what felt like hours in his mind. There was a man sitting at the table holding a drink in his hand. This stranger knew the man's name and stood to introduce himself—it was the boy's teacher. This is the same man who set all the obstacles in motion when I began forming Malthus, and now he was somehow present at the most crucial moment in the man's spiritual life. Malthus missed the mark on this whole endeavour and just watched as the Heavenly Host orchestrated a plan that would spoil any chance at redeeming our position. There are no mere chances with the Enemy, He seeks to control everything, and this was no different. It was not an accident that the man was somehow led to the farmer for employment, and that he was hired for a job for which he had no previous experience. None of this was an accident, and Malthus should have seen this from the beginning and promptly informed me.

As they shook hands the teacher and the father made very intentional eye contact, the teacher nodding ever so slightly.

They both looked at each other as if they had finally solved a riddle, each saying to the other almost telepathically, "It was you the whole time." The teacher finally put a concrete face to the man for whom he was prompted to pray and sacrifice, and the man suddenly understood why things had changed in his soul in recent weeks.

The evening digressed and got even worse, it was full of friends sharing food and the laughter of children. The men chatted and shared stories until well after midnight, and the man and teacher made plans to reunite the following day. I will spare certain details of their conversation as they are too terrible even to write, but after all was said and done, the worst happened; the father went with his new friend to his first Confession of his adult life. All our efforts, all my guidance, all the sins and stains crawling out of his soul like maggots on a dead animal, everything was wiped clean with those terrifying words of absolution. (Remember, all of these events fall at the feet of Malthus, they could have been avoided and he must be blamed. It is *his* fault that we have now lost this man, and, as I will explain presently, we have lost his family as well.)

The man's act of confessing his sins was as repugnant as one could ever imagine. For the better part of an hour he sat there with one of those traditional priests of whom the Enemy is so fond (those who torture us). After confessing everything he possibly could, he was instructed to, among other things, begin one of those unbearable prayers that lasts nine days. It was a prayer to Monica, the woman behind that insufferable Doctor of Grace. (Again, I have explained how all this awful timing has been orchestrated in the Enemy's favour, right under Malthus' nose.) He was instructed to adopt a series of physical punishments to atone for his transgressions—not the lovely pretend punishments that so many of our favourite priests prescribe today, but *real* punishments—while at the same time offering this in conjunction with his prayers for the conversion of his wife and children. He finished his task and on the 10th day, it was the abominable commemoration of Augustine, her son, and he interceded as we have seen many times.

For a little over a month, the Bishop from Hippo did his worst amidst the wife's anguish and despair. This could have been a fruitful time for Malthus to drive the woman deeper off the cliff, but the complacent fool failed. With each passing day, annoying pulsations of grace chipped away at the mother's resolve. Little by little her heart softened, and she came to hate her husband less and hate her sins more. At night she even laid in bed, staring at her mobile phone, watching as each moment passed in a hopeless expectation that her spouse would call. She was a wreck, but she was no longer our sort of wreck. Her egotism faded and her tears changed in flavour from a sour self-pity to a sanguine sorrow. Like an arid garden being pummeled by an axe, her soul became soil and was prepared to accept the death of a grain of wheat. It was a desperate moment indeed.

The financial situation for the woman was unsustainable, and therefore she began the process of selling the home. Because of this she embarked on the arduous process of sifting through all their belongings in preparation for relocation. The fearful symmetry of what happened is so infuriating that it is a wonder I have not completely burst into flames. The date was October 7th... Yes, that feast commemorating the Woman and her Psalter. I told you that the orchestration on behalf of the General was relentless, well it seems the Woman could not resist taunting us yet again. On that day, the mother worked away at various boxes that had been hidden away for years. She discovered a box of old keepsakes. The woman opened the old dust covered box that contained a variety of useless trinkets. Most were harmless and nothing more than souvenirs, but some were very harmful indeed. First she discovered old cinema ticket stubs, things she had kept from her first instance of courtship with her husband. For the first time in many months she did not hate him, but instead thought of him as the man she had wanted to marry years prior. It gets much worse. From there she held in her hand various pictures from her childhood, which brought her to tears. She did not understand why, but it is clear now that she felt a great pang of guilt and loss at the person she once was. There is almost nothing worse than a grown person calling to mind the state of childishness that the Awesome and Terrible King clamours on about. At any rate, eventually she came to a long thin box that contained relics from her Sacraments. Her stomach wrenched into a tight knot and she felt as if she may hyperventilate. Shaking, she opened the box to see a once-lit Sacramental candle and an antique chain of prayer beads. She hastily grabbed the beads and stared at them.

Suddenly, she felt what can only be described as a white-hot burning sensation in her palm; it was not our sort of burning, but was instead that purifying burning the Enemy brings in his hatred for what we hold most dear. Attached to the chain was a medal of Benedict. She then looked back into the box of memories and discovered an image of her grandmother, the same woman of whom you have read in my correspondence with Malthus. The black and white image showed that insufferable saint presenting the very same prayer chain to the Father of the Roman Church at a time before the Council. He blessed the item which was now in the woman's hands. At the sight of this relic from an age that seemed as if it never truly existed, the woman wept bitterly. She wept in that fashion that the Terrible Name wept over his friend at the tomb. Water flooded from her eyes in a way it never had before. She held the image in her hand and stared at the grandmother she had been so fond of, covering it with tears of sorrow. Then, she said her first honest prayer since she was a little girl. But it was not just any prayer, no, it was a prayer of petition to the Woman! She did not even know how to properly pray the beads, but she prayed the basic prayers nonetheless, going through the damnable chain for two full rounds. During this time her whole life flashed before her eyes, every sin she could ever remember.

She was mystically transported to a different location, and stood there in the form of a small child, holding the hand of the Woman amongst a crowd. She looked up and saw Him hanging on the Tree. She immediately internalized all the Blood she saw dripping from His wounds and was convinced of her contribution to every laceration. During this horrifying episode she gave full permission to all the Heavenly forces to cleanse her and do the Enemy's bidding. The husband himself was also praying and asking for a sign that his prayers to Monica had worked. He received his answer and was prompted to call his wife and speak with her for the first time in weeks. The sound of her phone ringing may as well have been the sound of those bells we hate so much at the moment of the transformation of the Sacrament. She snapped out of her trance hastily and looked to see who was calling her. When she saw it was him, she began to laugh while tears still dripped down her face like the Blood from the Thorns. She answered, and for a brief moment there was a pregnant pause not unlike that moment of insurrection when Gabriel waited for the

Woman to respond to the Annunciation. The husband stumbled to say anything and the woman could wait no longer. Right away she went on weeping with joyful sorrow about how she loved him and forgave him. He exhaled and joined in the insufferable weeping while they both spewed on about the most nauseating emotions. She was so enamoured with the fool and hypnotized by the Enemy that she begged him to come immediately and take her to confess her sins. Within an hour, the wretched woman was just as pure and clean as the man! Gnashing of teeth indeed.

I fear that if I continue much longer, you will be so filled with rage that you might associate this mounting rage with me, rather than directing it rightly towards Malthus. But, we must accept the relevant details in order to justly condemn the idiotic devil with all the forces of Hell.

Because the father realized his headship in the home, and because he was unjustly taken from our grasps and into the Enemy's graces, he selfishly took his offspring back. His daughter fell into his arms with little to no resistance. The females are designed in a way that makes a continual entrapment of their souls very difficult when their patriarch intervenes. There is something so fickle about the women, and this girl was no different. When the father and mother came home after they had visited the priest, the daughter sat in her usual position on the living-room sofa, reading one of our books. The fetal-position had become her constant resting stance, as she sought to close herself off from the world and escape into her novels. At the moment her father walked into the room, holding her mother's hand, she was reading a highly sensualized passage describing a lustful affair between a vampire and a teenage girl. As she looked up and saw the man who months ago had ripped her heart from her chest, she melted. That bastard waltzed in there, upright and with authority, his state of grace taunting us like priestly vestments. He used a forgettable pet-name he had for her and said, "Missy, I love you, I'm sorry, I will spend the rest of my life honouring your mother and we will be a family again, better than ever before." Water once again dripped from the man's eyes, but his countenance did not change as it did when he wept in front of his daughter months prior. Furthermore there was something that the girl found admirable about his facial irrigation. The girl was so malleable that her Guardian drew her attention to a single drop of tear that fell off his chin and onto the floor. In her mind she saw the tears of Paul, a man converted from the blindness of sin. The man stood there like a repentant Apostle, and she leapt into his arms as she had done when she was a small child. She remarked how much more solid and athletic was his build, no doubt due to his physical job. She was like a child reborn in her father's arms; she too was lost to us.

As for the son, his conversion was not so immediate, although he did eventually break. Pornography usage causes anger in the souls of men, as it is ultimately a hatred of the natural order, and the abuse of oneself for sterile pleasures; it is for these reasons that we are so fond of its promulgation. Because of the rage that had been building in him since the separation—as is common in all adolescent boys in broken homes—the video habit worked as an accelerant for his temper. He had been uncharacteristically angry for some time, which combined with his new philosophical interests, turned him into somewhat of a "loose canon." This was another thing that Malthus should have used to our advantage, but again, he pushed the same old tactics too far. Anger in the soul causes a man to expend a significant amount of energy, which in turn causes fatigue. Malthus, the idiot, had so much fun causing greater anger in the son by launching an endless barrage of hedonism, that he pushed him over the edge. By the time his father came home, his soul was dangerously tired. He still hated his father and revelled in his new interests, but he had no resilience left to act out his anger, especially against his father who demonstrated a new sort of redemptive confidence. The father had already consulted the farmer and the teacher about this reality, and he was prepared to handle the disposition of his son upon their reunification. Rather than try and explain himself to his son, he merely told him that he was "sorry, and did not deserve his forgiveness," and that he would be "ready to talk whenever he wanted." This strategy on behalf of the father gave the son nothing new to hate him for; he could continue to wallow in his anger, or he could decide to move on. The "ball was in his court" as the humans say.

A week later, the father kept his son home from school for the day. The boy had grown to hate school, and since the humans were still persisting in hellishly expedient virus adoration, schools were for us a great breeding ground of insanity. In any case, the father had other plans for the boy, plans which he kept hidden at first. As they drove out of town in the early hours, he said to his son, "You know, school can be the worst." The son said nothing, but he slightly nodded his head and let out a small chuckle. Nothing else was said on the ride, but as the sun began to rise the boy noticed an irritating light shining in his eye; it was the orange sunlight reflecting off the metal Tree attached to the beads hanging from the rear-view mirror. It had been almost four months since the young man had recited those blasted prayers, and it stung his conscience to stare at the Lady's Psalter, clothed with the sun. The father had brought the boy to work on the farm, and as they arrived he said, "Work hard and I will give you a hundred bucks." For the rest of the day they simply worked, without saying more than a few words. As is the case when men work hard together—something we continue to stifle by pushing females into predominantly male industries—they develop a certain trust by a sort of osmosis. The father and son did not speak, but the rage in the son's soul began to relinquish. For the next few days he stayed out of school and they did the same, and by the end they even began to laugh and act like chums, it was painful to watch.

At the end of the week the farmer presented the young man with a package that had been left for him. Confused, he opened it to find a book inside, but not just any book, it was *The Book*. There was a folded piece of paper that had been slipped in between two pages near the end of the book. It was a letter from his former teacher, it read: "Small world, your dad and I are friends now, who would have thought? He told me things were rough, so I thought you might want this. I highlighted a passage on the page where you found this letter, it's about you and your dad. You are more like him than you think. Cheers, Mr. J."

He read the passage. Without explaining why, he told his father to bring him to the church on the way home. His father obliged, and within three quarters of an hour he found himself kneeling in front of an altar while his son whispered away his iniquity in that damnable closet of repentance. Upon his release from our captivity he knelt down beside his father. He opened The Book to the page marked by the instructor and asked his father to read it. "There was a man who had two sons, the younger one said to his father, 'Father, give me my share'..." When the father was done reading, they both stared in silence at the graphic hanging memorial of Golgotha. No words were necessary, we had lost two prodigal sons.

The whole family now attends the liturgy and was enrolled in the Habit of the Woman on the feast of her Conception. In reality, they are entirely out of our grasp and now under the Mother's Mantle, untouchable by any of our advances. They have taken their interior change so seriously that the man even reversed the neutering he underwent a decade previous, and they are now expecting a set of twins that they will surely baptize! They have moved their family into a rural setting, where the man continues to work with the farmer, and they have downsized and humbled their material life to the point where the mother is now home. Nearly all marital chaos and discord has ceased, and they now gather at the kitchen table of their small country-home, to recite the Lady's Psalter every evening. As I said, they are utterly lost.

In conclusion to this most painful report, we must resolve to not only punish Malthus, but he must be made an example. The tactics of the Enemy and his adherents must be analyzed and synthesized into a comprehensive teaching philosophy to form more competent devils in the future. It is my contention that with enough work and progress we may finally vanquish our adversaries and take the humans as our rightful property and possession. Until that fateful day comes, let us have our fun with the devil to blame. We deserve at least a bit of consolation to distract ourselves from the embarrassment he has caused. Once again: Malthus is to blame, not me.

Quelle E. Quirinus
Undersecretary
Psychological Warfare

Made in the USA
Columbia, SC
17 June 2022